POP.O.LiCiOUS CAKE POPS

BY JOEY DELLINO
with TONY DELLINO

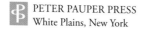

PETER PAUPER PRESS
White Plains, New York

DEDICATION

For my Mom, who introduced me to the art of crafts and gave me the love and passion for all things creative. You are my inspiration every single day. I love you and I miss you.

This book is dedicated to our three wonderful children: Andrew, Evan, and Joel. Thank you for your never-ending patience and for always being willing to eat the leftovers. We love you!

ACKNOWLEDGMENTS

- To my followers, fans, and blog readers: Thank you for all of your questions, comments, and endless support. Without you, this book would not have been possible.

- Mara Conlon, Barbara Paulding, Heather Zschock, and everyone at Peter Pauper Press: Thank you for absolutely everything, for being amazing partners to work with, and for helping push the limits of my creativity.

- To all of our family members: Thank you for your love and support.

- Jennifer Carver: For your unparalleled kindness and friendship, and for always being so supportive. Thank you for letting me be part of your amazing creations with Banner Events.

- Thank you to all of our friends and supporters in the blogging community: Meaghan Mountford (Craft Gossip/The Decorated Cookie), Kim Celano (KC Bakes), and everyone else who has supported us along the way.

POP.O.Licious
CaKe POPS

CONTENTS

INTRODUCTION

Do you have a sweet tooth? I do! From the time I was little, and even to this day, I've always been a sucker for the sweets . . . lots of pun intended. I love how candy can take me back to my childhood and those summer bike rides to the candy store. This is why the very first time I came across a cake pop, I knew I found something special. It was like we were made for each other!

Before we go much further, I need to tell you that first and foremost I'm a busy wife and mom. I love to bake, and decorate desserts, but I'm not a professional. So if I can do this, you CAN do this! Believe it or not, my husband does most of the cooking and baking around our house. But I've always been passionate about hand-crafted projects, so the art of cake pops was simply the perfect way to combine my sweet tooth with my crafting talents. I make cake pops because I love to create. I love to just let my imagination take over and let the creative process do its thing.

My inspiration for making cake pops came from Angie Dudley (a.k.a. Bakerella). There is no question that she brought this popular dessert to the forefront and led the way for the enormous trend that followed right behind her. The day my husband brought home her *Cake Pops* book, I headed straight for the kitchen. I was amazed by all the things you could do with cake, candy, and sprinkles. So, I started to create, and after that, the rest is history.

In 2010, my husband and I founded **Pop.O.Licious Cake Pops**, and in 2011, I started my own cake pop blog called **Every Day Should Pop!** *(www.365cakepops.com).* More than just a blog, it became a way of life! I set out to make 365 cake pops—one for each day of the year. Nationally and internationally, each day is recognized for something and I challenged myself to come up with a themed cake pop to match each occasion. I drew inspiration from everywhere—and it was great because it gave my family something to smile about!

Making cake pops for the blog was a learning experience, and over time I vastly expanded my skills and decorating abilities. It showed me that the possibilities were endless with these tiny desserts. I also came to realize that my readers inspired me just as much as I inspired them. I received comments and questions from people from all over the world, and that kept me going, too. Every day was a new adventure. It really helped prepare me to write this book, and I am thrilled to be able to share these creations with you.

In these pages I will show you what cake pops are all about. They're cake balls on a stick, right? Sure. But they can be so much more! Prepare yourself to take cake pops to the next level. I will share with you some of my favorite designs, and techniques for creating some of the most adorable cake bites you'll ever find. I'll show you easy tricks to make it all a cinch. You'll be a cake pop pro before you know it.

My goal for this book is exactly the same as it was for my blog. I want to inspire your creativity, show you something you may have never seen before, and, of course, brighten your day. Enjoy and happy creating!

Love,

Joey

TIPS, TRICKS, & FAQ

The first rule about cake pops is that there are no rules! This book should be your guide to make all kinds of clever creations. Let your imagination run wild and feel free to substitute your own decoration and candy preferences with whatever you'd like. If you don't like jelly beans, use an M&M, or anything else your heart desires. The purpose of my pops is to inspire your own imagination, so don't be afraid to do your own thing.

As you begin to tackle each cake pop, be sure to read the directions all the way through first. Try to get the full understanding of the process, gather your tools and ingredients, and then have at it. Be patient, be creative, but most importantly, have fun!

One of the best pieces of advice that I can give you is to always be prepared. Make sure you have your supplies and everything within reach, because most of the time you'll have to move quickly once you get going. Get your candy coating ready, count out any candies needed, and pull together the decorating tools that are called for. I'm here to help, so on the next few pages are my most commonly used tips, tricks, and answers to frequently asked questions.

FUN WITH CANDY COATINGS

How do I thin my candy coating wafers and get them to be a smooth consistency?

Two words: paramount crystals. This ingredient can be a lifesaver and can turn a gloppy mess of melted candy into a beautiful sheen of candy coating. Start with a little. Less is more because you can always add more in later. Melt the paramount crystals in the microwave in the same bowl with the candy coating. Stir to get your desired results. I use a regular metal spoon to stir the candy coating with quick and steady strokes. Oil or shortening will also thin your candy coating; however, they can often create a greasy end result and add unwanted flavor to the candy coating. I have never had these problems with paramount crystals.

Sometimes the candy coating can get overheated. Be sure to follow the instructions on the package and heat it at 30-second intervals. Make 'n Mold, Merkens, and Wilton are all good sources for candy coating in a variety of colors. However, all will melt at their own consistency, so the amount of paramount crystals needed to thin will also vary.

After you have melted the candy coating, and as you begin to work on the cake pops, the candy coating may re-harden quickly, or slowly, depending on the particular climate in your kitchen. Pay attention to the consistency and adjust it as needed. For example, as the uncoated cake pops are chilling in the refrigerator for

15 minutes, the melted candy coating in the bowl may re-harden. Make sure it is returned to a smooth consistency before dipping the cake pops. Microwave in very short intervals and stir.

Candy Coating—The Essential "Glue"

For nearly every project in this book, you'll need to attach some decorative elements to the cake pops (eyes, antlers, various candies, etc.). Sometimes you may be able to do this immediately after you've dipped the entire cake pop into the candy coating and it is still wet. But more often than not, you will need to use additional melted candy coating as the "glue" to attach these elements because the initial layer of coating will have hardened. Use the tip of a toothpick or lollipop stick to dab on candy coating "glue" wherever is needed.

Keep it on the Stick

Why do my cake pops keep falling off the stick?

Before putting the cake ball on the stick, the first thing you must do is dip the lollipop stick into the melted candy coating, and then insert it in the cake ball. This is an important step because the melted candy will act as the glue and allows the cake ball to hold onto the stick.

Also, make sure that the cake balls have been chilled. I recommend refrigerating cake pops for about 15 minutes or so after inserting the stick into the cake ball before proceeding. Otherwise, they have the tendency to soften up and fall apart when they get dipped.

If you've done all that and it still keeps falling off, another problem can be the size or weight of the cake ball itself. If it's too large or particularly dense with too much frosting, this can also cause the cake to fall off the stick. Tempting as it may be to add more frosting, be careful not to overdo it!

crumbling the cake & mixing the frosting

Do I have to use frosting as the binder for the cake pop?

After you've made your cake, the whole trick is turning it into little balls. There are a few methods to do this which require crumbling the cake and mixing in frosting. I recommend making cake pops with frosting in order to mold and shape them in the ways you'll see in this book. The cake has to have some kind of malleability and has to be able to bend and shape in a certain way. There are a lot of cake pop methods out there that don't require any frosting to create the ball, and those are fine for what they are. But to have success decorating and designing in the ways I'll demonstrate, you'll have to incorporate frosting into the ball to give it stability and let it hold its shape.

My preferred method of crumbling the cake is with a stand mixer. The most effective way to do this is by cutting your cake into manageable squares right in the cake pan and then dumping them into the bowl of the stand mixer. Start with half of the cake, crumble it, and then add more as you go along. After that, add the frosting to the crumbled cake. You'll need about half of a jar of store-bought frosting for one boxed cake mix recipe, or more or less depending how you like it. Add in the frosting to the cake and mix until it reaches a dough-like consistency.

This same process can be done with a hand mixer, or even by hand. However, I find that the stand mixer is the most effective and efficient way to do this with much less mess to clean up later.

cracking

Why do my cake pops keep cracking?

Cracking will occur usually because the cake balls have either been rolled too tight or because they are too cold. If the cake pops have been placed in the freezer, be sure to give them a little time to warm back up before dipping into the candy coating. To salvage a cracked cake pop, you can pipe on melted chocolate over the crack or smooth over with a toothpick. Also, you can try double-dipping your cake pop to hide the cracks. If none of that works, of course you can start all over and adjust to more manageable temperatures.

Leakage & Air Bubbles
Why do my cake pops leak oil?

A cake pop will leak because air bubbles have formed when you dipped the cake pop. If air bubbles creep to the surface of the cake pop they'll break open when the chocolate dries, creating small holes and exposing the cake ball underneath. They're often tiny holes the size of a pin, but they're still big enough that oil will seep out.

To avoid oil leakage or air bubbles altogether, tap the bowl against the counter, after the candy coating has been melted and stirred, so that all of the air bubbles come to the surface. At this point they'll usually pop and you won't have any issues. It is also very important to cover the entire cake ball completely when you dip it into the candy coating.

Edible Color Pens
Are all edible color pens the same?

Many of my recipes call for "edible color pens." I've had the best success with AmeriColor Gourmet Writer Food Decorating Pens. They last the longest and offer the best quality of all the pens I've ever tried. Writing on cake pops can be an art, and to create the best designs you'll need to have the best pens. Never press too hard when using an edible color pen. Always press lightly in thin short strokes. It sometimes helps to gently wipe off the tip with a paper towel.

TOOLS

To make cake pops, you'll need to have a few key items on hand. Most are common things already found around the kitchen, but a few may require a trip to a specialty shop or an online store. Be sure to keep a full supply of lollipop sticks and toothpicks on hand at all times.

- Cake pans
- Stand mixer
- Hand mixer
- Cookie scoop
- Microwave
- Microwave-safe bowls
- Food scale
- Lollipop sticks (either 4" or 6" length)
- Food-safe paintbrush
- Edible color pens
- Squeeze bottles
- Decorating bags, tips, & couplers
- Candy molds
- Cookie cutters
- Toothpicks
- Wax paper
- Cookie sheets
- Styrofoam block (large enough to stand your cake pops in to dry)
- Wood block cake pops stand (any size 3/4"–1" thick, with several 3/8" holes drilled in it)

ingredients

The most important thing about making cake pops is to make them fun, make them unique, and make them your own! The ingredients listed in each recipe should be used as a guide. If you don't have a certain candy item on hand, feel free to substitute it for something else that will work. I won't tell!

- Cake
- Frosting
- Candy coating
- Paramount crystals
- Candy
- Sprinkles

resources & suppliers

- Ateco *www.atecousa.net*
- County Kitchen SweetArt
  www.countrykitchensa.com
- Jo-Ann Fabric and Craft Stores *www.joann.com*
- KC Bakes Cake Pop Stands *www.kcbakes.com*
- Make 'n Mold *www.makenmold.com*
- Michaels *www.michaels.com*
- Williams-Sonoma *www.williams-sonoma.com*
- Wilton *www.wilton.com*

BASIC CAKE POPS RECIPE

MAKES APPROXIMATELY 36–40 CAKE POPS*

Cake pops are a fun and delicious treat. The creative options are endless and there is no limit to what you can do with these little dessert bites. But sometimes the basic round cake ball is more than enough to brighten someone's day.

Use this process to begin all of your cake pop projects, and then continue on to each recipe for the decorating instructions.

The number of cake pops this recipe yields depends on how large or small you make your cake balls. I recommend using a cookie scoop to make the balls a more consistent size. The rest of the projects in this book are designed to create 24 decorated cake pops, using this basic cake pop recipe as the starting point. Even though this recipe will yield more than 24 cake balls, it's always a good idea to have extras on hand when decorating, in case you run into any cracking/breaking problems and have to do some over.

WHAT YOU'LL NEED

18.25 oz. box cake mix, any flavor
9" x 13" cake pan
16 oz. container store-bought frosting
Cookie scoop (about 1-1/2" diameter)
32-oz. bag of candy coating, any flavor
48 lollipop sticks
Sprinkles, any color
Styrofoam or wooden block

WHAT TO DO

1. Bake the cake, following the instructions on the box, using a 9" x 13" cake pan. Let it cool completely and gather the rest of your supplies.

2. Cut the cake into 16 equal pieces while still in the cake pan. This will make it easier to crumble the cake in the electric mixer. Place 8 pieces into the bowl of the mixer and turn on at medium speed. Mix for 1 to 2 minutes until the cake is completely crumbled.

3. Add the remaining half of the cake to the bowl and continue mixing for another 1 to 2 minutes.

4. Add about half of the container of frosting (or 8 oz.) to the crumbled cake. Mix for 1 to 2 minutes until everything is completely mixed together and the cake reaches a dough-like consistency. Depend-

ing on how moist you want your cake pops, you
may want to add more frosting.

5. Use the cookie scoop to create the cake balls. (The
    cookie scoop will help to keep your cake pops con-
    sistent in size.) Remove the dough from the scoop
    and finish rounding them by hand. Place them all
    on a plate or cookie sheet lined with wax paper.

NOTE: At this point, if you are proceeding with another cake pop project in this book, see the specified
instructions for that cake pop and proceed as directed.

6. Place the candy coating in a microwave-safe bowl.
    Melt in the microwave, following the instructions on
    the package. Stir until you get a smooth consistency.

7. Dip the tip of a lollipop stick into the candy coat-
    ing about a half inch. Insert dipped end of stick
    into a cake ball, about halfway through the ball.
    Place ball on a plate or cookie sheet lined with wax
    paper (the lollipop stick should be vertical). Repeat
    with remaining cake balls.

8. Place the uncoated round cake pops in the refrig-
    erator for about 15 minutes before coating. This
    will give the pops time to firm up.

9. Remove the cake pops from the refrigerator. Dip a
    cake pop into the candy coating. (If the candy coat-
    ing has become too thick for dipping, re-melt it

slightly.) Once completely covered, pull the cake pop out and gently tap the stick on the edge of the bowl to allow excess candy coating to drip off. Place in a Styrofoam or wooden stand. As the pop coating begins to harden, but is still slightly soft, apply your favorite sprinkles over the pop. Repeat with remaining cake pops.

10. Let pops stand and dry completely.

General Cake Pop Tips

• Additional tools to have on hand for every cake pop project: microwave-safe bowls, Styrofoam or wooden block, toothpicks, spoon, extra lollipop sticks, and wax paper

• Cake pops can be made from any cake flavor and any cake recipe. I find box cake mixes make the most consistent pops and always give you predictable results.

• Crumbling the cake can be done several different ways. I find it easiest to use a stand mixer. However, you can also use a hand mixer or it can all be done by hand.

• If there are not specific melting instructions included on your candy coating package, just remember to microwave the candy coating in short intervals, about 20 seconds, stirring in between—making sure not to overheat.

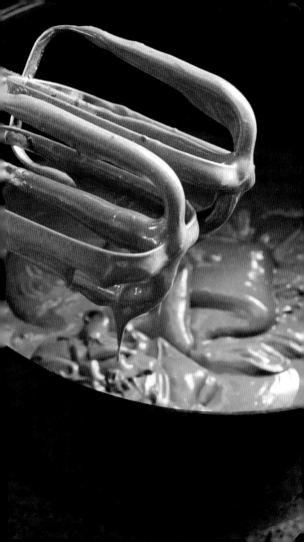

HOLiDAYS

• • • • • • • • • • • •

No holiday celebration is complete without the added joy of adorable cake pops! Go ahead and mix it up at the dessert table this year. Create something fun that will have the whole party talking. The kids will ask for seconds and everyone will want to know your secrets.

Scare things up for your Halloween trick-or-treaters with **Spooky Spider** cake pops. Or introduce a new family tradition to your Thanksgiving table with **Cornucopias**. You'll have Christmas party-goers delighting in the sight of the **Tangled Balls of Lights**. And everyone will be *oohing* and *ahhing* over the charming **Easter Bunnies** and **Hatching Chicks** pops! Your holiday traditions will never be the same!

PUMPKIN BUCKETS

MAKES 24 CAKE POPS

These candy-filled cake pops bring in quite the haul!

WHAT YOU'LL NEED

24 uncoated round cake balls
1 14- or 16-oz. bag orange candy coating
24 lollipop sticks
2 black licorice pinwheels
Black edible color pen
Flower sprinkles

WHAT TO DO

1. Prepare the uncoated round cake balls *(see basic pop recipe on page 21)*.

2. Place the candy coating in a microwave-safe bowl. Melt in the microwave, following the instructions on the package. Stir until you get a smooth consistency.

3. Dip the tip of a lollipop stick into the candy coating about a half inch. Insert dipped end of stick into a cake ball, about halfway through the ball. Place ball on a plate or cookie sheet lined with wax paper. Repeat with remaining cake balls.

4. Chill the cake pops in refrigerator (for about 15 minutes).

5. Unroll the black licorice pinwheel and cut into 24 pieces (2" each), for the handles. Set aside.

6. Remove the cake pops from the refrigerator. Dip a cake pop into the candy coating. Once completely covered, pull the cake pop out and gently tap the stick on the edge of the bowl to allow the excess candy coating to drip off. Place in a stand and let dry completely. Repeat with remaining cake pops.

7. Dip the tip of a toothpick into the candy coating and dab 2 dots onto the top of a cake pop on opposite sides. This will be the glue for the base of the bucket handles. Bend a licorice piece in your hand before placing on the pop to help it set and maintain its shape as it dries. Place ends on the top of the cake pop, into the candy coating dots, arching over the top. Hold until dry. Repeat with remaining cake pops.

8. Draw on the eyes, nose, and mouth for each of the cake pops with the black edible color pen.

9. Dip the tip of a toothpick in the candy coating and dab on the top of a cake pop. This will be the glue for the flower sprinkles. Attach the flower sprinkles and let dry. Repeat with remaining cake pops.

10. Shade the top of each of the cake pops in front of the sprinkles with the black edible color pen.

11. Let stand and dry completely.

CRAZY CANDY CORN

MAKES 24 CAKE POPS

These adorable candy corn cake pops are ready to be the life of any party!

WHAT YOU'LL NEED

24 uncoated cake triangles *(shaping instructions below)*
1 14- or 16-oz. bag yellow candy coating
24 lollipop sticks
2 black licorice pinwheels
1 14- or 16-oz. bag orange candy coating
1 14- or 16-oz. bag white candy coating
Black edible color pen
Candy pumpkins (optional)
Cream-filled chocolate cookies (optional)
Hershey Kisses (optional)
Black sprinkles (optional)

WHAT TO DO

1. Prepare the uncoated cake triangles by first rolling out all of the individual balls for the basic cake pops *(see page 21)*. Then shape each ball into a triangle by pinching each one in between your thumb and forefinger to create a narrow

top and flattened base. Place them all on a plate or cookie sheet lined with wax paper.

2. Place the yellow candy coating in a microwave-safe bowl. Melt in the microwave, following the instructions on the package. Stir until you get a smooth consistency.

3. Dip the tip of a lollipop stick into the yellow candy coating about a half inch. Insert dipped end of stick into the bottom of a cake triangle, making sure it is inserted far enough to achieve stability. Place triangle on a plate or cookie sheet lined with wax paper. Repeat with remaining cake triangles.

4. Chill the cake pops in refrigerator (for about 15 minutes).

5. Unroll the black licorice pinwheel and cut into 48 pieces (1 to 1-1/2" each), and set aside.

6. Place the orange and white candy coating in separate microwave-safe bowls. Melt in the microwave, following the instructions on the package. Stir until you get a smooth consistency.

7. Remove the cake pops from the refrigerator. Dip a cake pop into the yellow candy coating. Once completely covered, pull the cake pop out and gently tap the stick on the edge of the bowl to allow the excess candy coating to drip off. Place in a stand

and let dry completely. Repeat with remaining cake pops.

8. Dip the top 2/3 of a cake pop into the orange candy coating. Once the top portion is completely covered, pull the cake pop out and gently tap the stick on the edge of the bowl to allow the excess candy coating to drip off. Place in a stand and let dry completely. Repeat with remaining cake pops.

9. Dip the top 1/3 of a cake pop into the white candy coating. Once the top portion is completely covered, pull the cake pop out and gently tap the stick on the edge of the bowl to allow the excess candy coating to drip off. Place in a stand and let dry completely. Repeat with remaining cake pops.

10. Draw on the eyes, eyebrows, nose, and mouth for each of the cake pops, with the black edible color pen. Dip the tip of a toothpick into the white candy coating and dot the center of the eyes.

11. Gently poke a hole in each side of a pop with a toothpick deep enough so the licorice arms will stay on their own. Insert the licorice pieces and bend to shape the arms. Repeat with remaining cake pops.

12. Let pops stand and dry completely.

TIPS

You can give each candy corn character its own personality by drawing different silly, spooky, scary faces, or by adding accessories!

* To attach the candy pumpkin, first cut the pumpkin in half so it will adhere easily. Dip a toothpick in candy coating and dab onto the center of the pop, below the face. Place the pumpkin and hold until dry. Then dab more candy coating onto the front of the pumpkin and bend one of the arms around to the front, attaching it to the front of the pumpkin. Hold until dry.

* Add a witch's hat *(see hat instructions on page 50).*

DRACULAS

MAKES 24 CAKE POPS

I vant to eat this cake pop!

WHAT YOU'LL NEED

24 uncoated round cake balls
1 14- or 16-oz. bag white candy coating
1 14- or 16-oz. bag black candy coating
4-oz. squeeze bottle
Black edible color pen
Red edible color pen
Peach edible color pen
24 strands of purple ribbon (about 7" each)

WHAT TO DO

1. Prepare the uncoated round cake balls *(see basic pop recipe on page 21)*.

2. Place the white candy coating in a microwave-safe bowl. Melt in the microwave, following the instructions on the package. Stir until you get a smooth consistency.

3. Dip the tip of a lollipop stick into the candy coating about a half inch. Insert dipped end of stick into a cake ball, about halfway through the ball. Place ball on a plate or cookie sheet lined with wax paper. Repeat with remaining cake balls.

4. Chill the cake pops in refrigerator (for about 15 minutes).

5. Remove the cake pops from the refrigerator. Dip a cake pop into the white candy coating. Once completely covered, pull the cake pop out and gently tap the stick on the edge of the bowl to allow the excess candy coating to drip off. Place in a stand and let dry completely. Repeat with remaining cake pops.

6. Place the black candy coating in a separate microwave-safe bowl. Melt in the microwave, following the instructions on the package. Stir until you get a smooth consistency.

7. Fill the squeeze bottle with the black candy coating. Pipe the black candy coating on the top of a cake pop, creating the hairline down the side and widow's peak first. Once you have established the hairline, fill in the rest behind it to create the full head of hair. Repeat with remaining cake pops. If the candy coating begins to harden in the bottle, just microwave it slightly, making it smooth enough to pipe. Let cake pops dry.

8. Draw on the eyes, eyebrows, nose, mouth, and fangs with the black edible color pen. Draw two drops of blood with the red edible color pen. Dab the peach edible color pen on the cheeks and smear

slightly with your finger. Repeat with remaining cake pops.

9. Dip the tip of a toothpick into the white candy coating and dot the center of all of the eyes.

10. Let pops stand and dry completely.

11. Tie a ribbon around the lollipop stick at the base of the head, and repeat with remaining cake pops.

TIP

• You can also dab a bit of pink luster dust on the cake pops to create the same effect for the cheeks.

FRANKENSTEINS

MAKES 24 CAKE POPS

*The kids will scream in delight when they
see Frankenstein at this year's party!*

WHAT YOU'LL NEED

24 uncoated cake rectangles *(shaping instructions
   below)*
1 14- or 16-oz. bag green candy coating
24 lollipop sticks
1 black licorice pinwheel
Black jimmie sprinkles
48 candy eyes
Black edible color pen

WHAT TO DO

1. Prepare the uncoated
   cake rectangles by first
   rolling out all of the individual balls for the
   basic cake pops *(see page
   21)*. Then shape each
   ball into a rectangle by
   flattening each one
   slightly between your
   hands. Mold each one into a rectangle with a ta-
   pered end for the base of the pop. Place them all

on a plate or cookie sheet lined with wax paper.

2. Place the candy coating in a microwave-safe bowl. Melt in the microwave, following the instructions on the package. Stir until you get a smooth consistency.

3. Dip the tip of a lollipop stick into the candy coating about a half inch. Insert dipped end of stick into the bottom of a cake rectangle, making sure it is inserted far enough to achieve stability. Place rectangle on a plate or cookie sheet lined with wax paper. Repeat with remaining cake rectangles.

4. Chill the cake pops in refrigerator (for about 15 minutes).

5. Unroll the black licorice pinwheel and cut into 48 pieces (1/2" each). Set aside.

6. Remove the cake pops from the refrigerator. Dip a cake pop into the candy coating. Once completely covered, pull the cake pop out and gently tap the stick on the edge of the bowl to allow the excess candy coating to drip off. Place in a stand and let dry completely. Repeat with remaining cake pops.

7. Re-dip the top half-inch of a cake pop into the candy coating to create a straight edge for the hairline. Pour the black jimmie sprinkles onto the

candy coating over a bowl and let dry. Repeat with remaining cake pops.

8. Dip the tip of a toothpick into the candy coating and apply two dabs on the face where the eyes will go. Attach the candy eyes on the dabs of candy coating to adhere them.

9. Dip the tip of a toothpick into the candy coating and apply to the cake pop on the sides at the base. Attach a licorice piece on each side and hold until dry. Repeat steps 8 and 9 with remaining cake pops.

10. Draw on the mouth and scar for each of the cake pops with the black edible color pen.

11. Let pops stand and dry completely.

SPOOKY SPIDERS

MAKES 24 CAKE POPS

*Grab these spooky spider cake pops
before they crawl away!*

WHAT YOU'LL NEED

24 uncoated round cake balls
1 14- or 16-oz. bag black candy coating
24 lollipop sticks
48 candy eyes
Black jimmie sprinkles
3 black licorice pinwheels

WHAT TO DO

1. Prepare the uncoated round cake balls *(see basic pop recipe on page 21)*.

2. Place the candy coating in a microwave-safe bowl. Melt in the microwave, following the instructions on the package. Stir until you get a smooth consistency.

3. Dip the tip of a lollipop stick into the candy coating about a half inch. Insert dipped end of stick into a cake ball, about halfway through the ball. Place ball on a plate or cookie sheet lined with wax paper. Repeat with remaining cake balls.

4. Chill the cake pops in refrigerator (for about 15 minutes).

5. Remove the cake pops from the refrigerator. Dip a cake pop into the candy coating. Once completely covered, pull the cake pop out and gently tap the stick on the edge of the bowl to allow the excess candy coating to drip off.

6. As the pop begins to harden, but is still slightly soft, place two candy eyes on for the face. Immediately after, apply black sprinkles all over the ball until covered. Stand the pop on the wax paper with the stick facing upward and let dry completely. Repeat with remaining cake pops.

7. Unroll the black licorice pinwheels and cut into 3-1/2" to 4" pieces for the legs (8 legs per pop).

8. After the pop dries completely, use a toothpick to gently poke eight holes toward the top where the legs will be inserted. Make the holes deep enough so that the licorice can stay on its own. Insert and curl the legs as shown in the photograph. Repeat with remaining cake pops.

WITCHES

*You'll be willing to endure a witch's spell just to
get your hands on one of these cake pops!*

WHAT YOU'LL NEED

24 uncoated round cake balls
24 lollipop sticks
1 14- or 16-oz. bag green candy coating
1 14- or 16-oz. bag black candy coating
4-oz. squeeze bottle
Black edible color pen
Small handful of white candy coating wafers
12 cream-filled chocolate cookies
24 Hershey's Kisses
Light corn syrup
Food-safe paintbrush
Black sprinkles

WHAT TO DO

1. Prepare the uncoated round cake balls *(see basic pop
   recipe on page 21).*

2. Place the green candy coating in a microwave-safe
   bowl. Melt in the microwave, following the instructions on the package. Stir until you get a smooth
   consistency.

3. Dip the tip of a lollipop stick into the green candy coating about a half inch. Insert dipped end of stick into a cake ball, about halfway through the ball. Place ball on a plate or cookie sheet lined with wax paper. Repeat with remaining cake balls.

4. Chill the cake pops in refrigerator (for about 15 minutes).

5. Remove the cake pops from the refrigerator. Dip a cake pop into the green candy coating. Once completely covered, pull the cake pop out and gently tap the stick on the edge of the bowl to allow the excess candy coating to drip off. Place in a stand and let dry completely. Repeat with remaining cake pops.

6. Place the black candy coating in a separate microwave-safe bowl. Melt in the microwave, following the instructions on the package. Stir until you get a smooth consistency.

7. Fill the squeeze bottle with the black candy coating. Pipe the black candy coating on the top of a cake pop, creating the hairline down the sides first. Once you have established the hairline, fill in the rest behind it to create the full head of hair. Let stand and dry completely. Repeat with remaining cake pops.

8. Dip the tip of a toothpick into the green candy coating and dab it in the center of a cake pop to create the nose. Repeat with remaining cake pops.

9. Draw on the eyes, eyebrows, and mouth for each of the cake pops with the black edible color pen.

10. Place the white candy coating wafers in a separate microwave-safe bowl. Melt in the microwave, following the instructions on the package. Stir until you get a smooth consistency.

11. Dip the tip of a toothpick into the white candy coating and dot the center of all of the eyes.

12. Create the hat: Separate the chocolate wafer ends from the cream-filled cookie. Squeeze a dab of black candy coating on top of the cake pop where you will attach the chocolate wafer. Squeeze another dab of black candy coating on top of the wafer in the center. Place the Hershey's Kiss on top. Lightly brush light corn syrup to coat the Hershey's Kiss, and cover with the black sprinkles. Repeat with remaining cake pops.

13. Let pops stand and dry completely.

CORNUCOPIAS

MAKES 24 CAKE POPS

Cornucopia cake pops are perfect accent pieces for any dessert tray and will leave your guests asking for seconds!

WHAT YOU'LL NEED

24 uncoated cake horn shapes *(shaping instructions below)*
1 14- or 16-oz. bag dark chocolate candy coating
24 lollipop sticks
3 oz. shredded coconut
12 candy pumpkins
Fruit-shaped candy

WHAT TO DO

1. Prepare the uncoated cake horn shapes by first rolling out all of the individual balls for the basic cake pops *(see page 21)*. Then shape each ball into a horn  shape by pinching each one in between your thumb and forefinger to taper the pointed end, tilting it upward. Flatten the wide round end. Place them all on a plate or cookie sheet lined with wax paper.

2. Place the candy coating in a microwave-safe bowl. Melt in the microwave, following the instructions on the package. Stir until you get a smooth consistency.

3. Dip the tip of a lollipop stick into the candy coating about a half inch. Insert dipped end of stick into the base of a cake horn shape, about an inch behind the flattened, round end. Make sure it is inserted far enough to achieve stability. Place horn on a plate or cookie sheet lined with wax paper. Repeat with remaining cake horn shapes.

4. Chill the cake pops in refrigerator (for about 15 minutes).

5. Remove the cake pops from the refrigerator. Dip a cake pop into the candy coating. Once completely covered, pull the cake pop out and gently tap the stick on the edge of the bowl to allow the excess candy coating to drip off. Place in a stand and let dry completely. Repeat with remaining cake pops.

6. Spread the shredded coconut out evenly on an oven-safe baking sheet. Toast the coconut at 350° for about 5 minutes, or until golden brown. Remove from oven and let cool for 3 to 4 minutes before using.

7. Re-dip the flat side of a pop into the candy coating. Sprinkle the toasted coconut around the base so

that it sticks and is coated all the way around. Repeat with remaining cake pops.

8. Cut the mini pumpkin candies in half to make them easier to attach to the cake pop. Dip the tip of a toothpick into the candy coating, and spread on the flat side of the pop. Then attach the pumpkin and hold in place until it is set. Repeat this same procedure to apply the fruit-shaped candy all around the pumpkin. Repeat with remaining cake pops.

9. Let pops stand and dry completely.

MAKES 24 CAKE POPS

*These turkey cake pops will quickly become a new
Thanksgiving tradition when dessert rolls around!*

WHAT YOU'LL NEED

24 uncoated cake ovals *(shaping instructions below)*
1 14- or 16-oz. bag dark chocolate candy coating
24 lollipop sticks
120 Swedish Fish
24 yellow triangle sprinkles*
24 red candy-coated chocolate sunflower seeds
48 mini brown candy-coated chocolates
48 flower sprinkles
48 white nonpareils
Black edible color pen

WHAT TO DO

1. Prepare the uncoated cake
   ovals by first rolling out all
   of the individual balls for
   the basic cake pops *(see page
   21)*. Then shape each ball
   into an oval by gently
   squeezing in one hand and
   turning slightly to create the
   oval. Place them all on a

plate or cookie sheet lined with wax paper.

2. Place the candy coating in a microwave-safe bowl. Melt in the microwave, following the instructions on the package. Stir until you get a smooth consistency.

3. Dip the tip of a lollipop stick into the candy coating about a half inch. Insert dipped end of the stick into the wide base of a cake oval, making sure it is inserted far enough to achieve stability. Place oval on a plate or cookie sheet lined with wax paper. Repeat with remaining cake ovals.

4. Chill the cake pops in refrigerator (for about 15 minutes).

5. Remove the cake pops from the refrigerator. Dip the cake pop into the candy coating. Once completely covered, pull the cake pop out and gently tap the stick on the edge of the bowl to allow the excess candy coating to drip off. Place in a stand and let dry completely. Repeat with remaining cake pops.

6. Dab a small amount of candy coating onto wax paper with a spoon. Spread it into a circle about the size of a quarter. Arrange five Swedish Fish over the candy coating and fan out.

These will be the feathers. You may need to cut the tail off of the center fish so they all fit and don't overlap. Let sit for a few minutes and harden completely. Repeat with remaining fish.

7. With a spoon, drizzle a thin line of candy coating down the center of the back of a cake pop. This will act as the glue for the feathers.

8. Press the back of the cake pop with the wet candy coating against the hardened chocolate still holding the Swedish Fish on the wax paper. Let sit for 2 to 3 minutes, allowing time for the pop to adhere before continuing to the next step.

9. Once the cake pop is secure, gently peel away from the wax paper. Repeat steps 7 through 9 with remaining cake pops.

10. Dip the tip of a toothpick in the candy coating and dab a small amount on the front of the cake pop, slightly above center. Attach the triangle sprinkle for the nose.

11. Using the same technique in step 10, dab candy coating on the cake pop and place the red candy-coated chocolate sunflower seed for the wattle, the mini brown candy-coated chocolates for the wings, the flower sprinkles for the feet, and the white nonpareils for the eyes. Repeat steps 10 and 11 with remaining cake pops.

12. With the black edible color pen, draw small dots on each of the white nonpareils to create pupils on the eyes.

13. Let pops stand and dry completely.

TIP
• Classic cake pop turkeys often call for candy corn to be used for the feathers, which is a nice alternative.

I used triangle sprinkles made by Wilton, but feel free to substitute with another shape if you'd like!

TANGLED BALLS OF LIGHTS

MAKES 24 CAKE POPS

Putting up the Christmas lights can often give you a headache, but these tangled lights will put a smile on your face!

WHAT YOU'LL NEED

24 uncoated round cake balls
1 14- or 16-oz. bag green candy coating
24 lollipop sticks
3 oz. candy-coated chocolate sunflower seeds
4-oz. squeeze bottle

WHAT TO DO

1. Prepare the uncoated round cake balls *(see basic pop recipe on page 21)*.

2. Place the candy coating in a microwave-safe bowl. Melt in the microwave, following the instructions on the package. Stir until you get a smooth consistency.

3. Dip the tip of a lollipop stick into the candy coating about a half inch. Insert dipped end of stick into a cake ball, about halfway through the ball. Place ball on a plate or cookie sheet lined with wax paper. Repeat with remaining cake balls.

4. Chill the cake pops in refrigerator (for about 15 minutes).

5. Remove the cake pops from the refrigerator. Dip a cake pop into the candy coating. Once completely covered, pull the cake pop out and gently tap the stick on the edge of the bowl to allow the excess candy coating to drip off. Place in a stand.

6. As the pop coating begins to harden, but is still slightly soft, place the sunflower seeds all over, sticking the rounded ends into the cake pop. Let dry completely. Repeat steps 5 and 6 with remaining cake pops.

7. Fill the squeeze bottle with the remaining candy coating. Pipe it onto the pop, swirling all over to get the look of a tangled cord. You may need to do this process a few times, letting each layer dry in between.

8. Let pops stand and dry completely.

TIP

• The candy coating should be cooled slightly when it gets put into the squeeze bottle. If it is too warm it will be runny and will not harden in the right shape.

RED-NOSED REINDEER

MAKES 24 CAKE POPS

A slightly different spin on everyone's favorite reindeer!

WHAT YOU'LL NEED

24 uncoated round cake balls
1 14- or 16-oz. bag dark chocolate candy coating
24 lollipop sticks
48 mini candy canes
48 candy eyes
24 red jelly beans
Black edible color pen
24 strands of red ribbon (about 7" each)

WHAT TO DO

1. Prepare the uncoated round cake balls *(see basic pop recipe on page 21)*.

2. Take 6 chocolate candy coating wafers and set them aside. (You will use these to create the ears in a later step.) Place the rest of the candy coating in a microwave-safe bowl. Melt in the microwave, following the instructions on the package. Stir until you get a smooth consistency.

3. Dip the tip of a lollipop stick into the candy coating about a half inch. Insert dipped end of stick

into a cake ball, about halfway through the ball. Place ball on a plate or cookie sheet lined with wax paper. Repeat with remaining cake balls.

4. Chill the cake pops in refrigerator (for about 15 minutes).

5. To create the ears, trim each of the reserved 6 chocolate wafers to about 1/2" tall, creating a flat end and a pointed end. Four ears can be made from one wafer. Set these aside.

6. Cut each of the mini candy canes into a "U" shape and set aside.

7. Remove the cake pops from the refrigerator. Dip a cake pop into the candy coating. Once completely covered, pull the cake pop out and gently tap the stick on the edge of the bowl to allow the excess candy coating to drip off. Place in a stand.

8. As the pop coating begins to harden, but is still slightly soft, place the U-shaped candy canes on top for the antlers. Hold in place until dry. Place the base of the ears on the pop in front of each of the candy canes. Attach the candy eyes and jelly bean for the nose. You may need to dab on more candy coating as glue if the pop hardens too quickly. Repeat steps 7 and 8 with remaining cake pops.

9. Once the pop coating hardens, draw on the mouth for each of the cake pops with the black edible color pen.

10. Let pops stand and dry completely.

11. Tie a ribbon around a lollipop stick at the base of the reindeer's head, and repeat with remaining cake pops.

TIPS

- When cutting chocolate wafers for the ears, use the edge of a round cookie cutter to ensure that you get the same shape for each one.

- Feel free to experiment using other decorative ingredients! Any round, red candy can be used for the nose. And mini pretzels, or chocolate-covered pretzels, can be used for the antlers.

SANTAS

*You better watch out, you better not cry.
Santa cake pops are here, that's the reason why!*

WHAT YOU'LL NEED

24 uncoated round cake balls
1 14- or 16-oz. bag peach candy coating
24 lollipop sticks, plus one extra to be used as a
    decorating tool
24 chocolate chips
1 14- or 16-oz. bag red candy coating
1 14- or 16-oz. bag white candy coating
24 white dragée sprinkles
Black edible color pen
Food-safe paintbrush
Red sparkle dust
4-oz. squeeze bottle (optional)

WHAT TO DO

1. Prepare the uncoated round cake balls *(see basic pop recipe on page 21)*.

2. Place the peach candy coating in a microwave-safe bowl. Melt in the microwave, following the instructions on the package. Stir until you get a smooth consistency.

3. Dip the tip of a lollipop stick into the peach candy coating about a half inch. Insert dipped end of stick into a cake ball, about halfway through the ball. Place ball on a plate or cookie sheet lined with wax paper. Repeat with remaining cake balls.

4. Chill the cake pops in refrigerator (for about 15 minutes).

5. Remove the cake pops from the refrigerator. Dip a cake pop into the peach candy coating. Once completely covered, pull the cake pop out and gently tap the stick on the edge of the bowl to allow the excess candy coating to drip off. Place in a stand.

6. As the pop coating begins to harden, but is still slightly soft, place a chocolate chip on top of the pop.* *(See tip on page 71.)* This will create the shape for the pointed hat *(as seen on the Santa pop on the left in the photo).* Repeat steps 5 and 6 with remaining cake pops, and let dry completely.

7. Place the red and white candy coating in separate microwave-safe bowls. Melt in the microwave, following the instructions on the package. Stir until you get a smooth consistency.

8. To create Santa's red hat, dip the top of a cake pop—with the chocolate chip firmly attached—into the red candy coating about a quarter of the

way down, completely covering the chip. Allow excess candy coating to drip off.

9. As the red candy coating dries, apply one dragée sprinkle to the end of the hat *(as seen on the Santa pop on the left in the photo)*. Repeat steps 8 and 9 with remaining cake pops, and let dry completely.

10. Use the end of the extra lollipop stick to apply the brim of the hat and beard. Dip the tip of the stick into the white candy coating about a half inch. Apply dabs of candy coating onto the hardened pop, texturizing to give the look of a beard and furry hat. Dab a bit of the candy coating onto the dragée sprinkle with the stick, re-dipping as needed to create the furry look. Repeat with remaining cake pops.

11. Draw the eyes and mouth on each of the cake pops with the black edible color pen.

12. Dip the tip of a toothpick into the peach candy coating and dab above the mouth to create the nose on each of the cake pops.

13. Dip the food-safe paintbrush into the red sparkle dust. Gently blot on a paper towel first, then dab onto the cheeks of each of the cake pops.

14. Dip the tip of a toothpick into the white candy coating and gently apply white coating over the

eyes and mouth to create the eyebrows and mustache. Dab the tip of the toothpick and dot the center of the eyes. Repeat with remaining cake pops.

15. Let pops stand and dry completely.

TIP

* To create a hat that drapes down around the side of the face, *(as seen on the Santa pop on the right in the photo)*, do not add the chocolate chip to the cake pop. Instead, dip the top of the cake pop into the red candy coating about a quarter of the way down and drip off excess. Then place some of the red candy coating into a small squeeze bottle and pipe the red candy coating down the side of the pop about 3/4 of an inch. Apply the dragée sprinkle as described in step 9.

SNOWMEN

MAKES 24 CAKE POPS

Snowmen get cold too, and even these cake pops had to bundle up with earmuffs and scarves!

WHAT YOU'LL NEED

24 uncoated round cake balls
1 14- or 16-oz. bag white candy coating
24 lollipop sticks
48 black crunch sprinkles
24 orange candy-coated chocolate sunflower seeds
48 gummy sour cherries
24 strands sour straw candy*
Black edible color pen
24 strands of ribbon (about 7" each) (any color)

WHAT TO DO

1. Prepare the uncoated round cake balls *(see basic pop recipe on page 21).*

2. Place the candy coating in a microwave-safe bowl. Melt in the microwave, following the instructions on the package. Stir until you get a smooth consistency.

*Haribo Sour Spaghetti candies are already pre-cut to the appropriate size. But if you can't find this specific brand, cut each sour straw candy into about 1-1/2" pieces.

3. Dip the tip of a lollipop stick into the candy coating about a half inch. Insert dipped end of stick into a cake ball, about halfway through the ball. Place ball on a plate or cookie sheet lined with wax paper. Repeat with remaining cake balls.

4. Chill the cake pops in refrigerator (for about 15 minutes).

5. Remove the cake pops from the refrigerator. Dip a cake pop into the white candy coating. Once completely covered, pull the cake pop out and gently tap the stick on the edge of the bowl to allow the excess candy coating to drip off. Place in a stand.

6. As the pop begins to harden, but is still slightly soft, attach the crunch sprinkles for the eyes, the orange sunflower seed for the nose, and the gummy sour cherries for the earmuffs. Repeat steps 5 and 6 with remaining cake pops.

7. Dip the tip of a toothpick into the white candy coating and dab it onto the ends of a sour spaghetti strand. Place the strand on top of the pop to connect the sour cherries. Peak it in the middle for added height. Repeat with remaining cake pops.

8. With the black edible color pen, draw dots for the mouth on each of the cake pops.

9. Tie a ribbon around a lollipop stick at the base of the snowman's head, and repeat with remaining cake pops.

10. Let pops stand and dry completely.

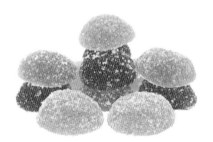

STOCKINGS

MAKES 24 CAKE POPS

*The stockings were hung by the chimney with care,
and these cake pops were made with festive flair!*

WHAT YOU'LL NEED

24 uncoated cake stockings *(shaping instructions below)*
1 14- or 16-oz. bag red candy coating
24 lollipop sticks
24 teddy bear crackers
Brown edible color pen
1 14- or 16-oz. bag green candy coating
1 14- or 16-oz. bag white candy coating
4-oz. squeeze bottle
12 mini candy canes (cut in half)
Crunch sprinkles
Flower sprinkles
Colored ball sprinkles

WHAT TO DO

1. Prepare the uncoated cake stockings by first rolling out all of the individual balls for the basic cake pops *(see page 21)*. Then shape each ball into a J-shape by flattening

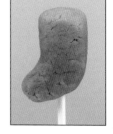

each ball slightly and pinching it with your thumb and forefinger. Place them all on a plate or cookie sheet lined with wax paper.

2. Place the red candy coating in a microwave-safe bowl. Melt in the microwave, following the instructions on the package. Stir until you get a smooth consistency.

3. Dip the tip of a lollipop stick into the red candy coating about a half inch. Insert dipped end of stick into the bottom of the stocking, making sure it is inserted far enough to achieve stability. Place stocking on a plate or cookie sheet lined with wax paper. Repeat with remaining cake stockings.

4. Chill the cake pops in refrigerator (for about 15 minutes).

5. Prepare the teddy bear crackers by cutting off the bottom halves of each. Then use the brown edible color pen to draw in the eyes, nose, and mouth for each. Set them aside.

6. Remove the cake pops from the refrigerator. Dip a cake pop into the red candy coating. Once completely covered, pull the cake pop out and gently tap the stick on the edge of the bowl to allow the excess candy coating to drip off. Place in a stand and let dry completely. Repeat with remaining cake pops.

7. Place the green and white candy coating in separate microwave-safe bowls. Melt them in the microwave, following the instructions on the package. Stir until you get a smooth consistency.

8. Fill the squeeze bottle with the green candy coating. Pipe it onto the toe of a cake pop. And then pipe it onto the heel, creating the look of a square patch. Let dry. Repeat with remaining cake pops.

9. Dip the top of a cake pop into the white candy coating about a half inch. Use the tip of a toothpick to texture the white candy coating and give it a fluffy appearance, adding more candy coating if needed.

10. As the pop hardens, but is still slightly soft, arrange the teddy bear, candy cane, and all the varied sprinkles on top of the cake pop. Use more white candy coating as glue if needed. Repeat steps 9 and 10 with remaining cake pops.

11. Dip the tip of a toothpick into the white candy coating and dot the center of each of the teddy bear eyes.

12. Let pops stand and dry completely.

TIP
• As an alternative, the stockings can be just one solid color. Or decorate them with polka dots or stripes!

WREATHS

*A classic Christmas wreath with a new twist—
you can eat these delectable decorations!*

WHAT YOU'LL NEED

24 uncoated cake wreaths *(shaping instructions below)*
1 14- or 16-oz. bag green candy coating
24 lollipop sticks
Candy cane sprinkles
Red sprinkles
Silver and gold dragée sprinkles
24 white chocolate chips
24 pieces of red licorice rope (7" each)

WHAT TO DO

1. Prepare the uncoated cake wreaths by first rolling
    out all of the individual balls for the basic cake pops
    (see page 21). Place them all on a plate or cookie
    sheet lined with wax paper. Then flatten each one
    slightly by just pressing down, using your hand or
    the bottom of a glass.

2. Place the candy coating in a microwave-safe bowl.
    Melt in the microwave, following the instructions
    on the package. Stir until you get a smooth consis-
    tency.

3. Dip the tip of a lollipop stick into the candy coating about a half inch. Insert dipped end of stick into the bottom of a cake wreath, making sure it is inserted far enough to achieve stability. Place wreath on a plate or cookie sheet lined with wax paper. Repeat with remaining cake wreaths.

4. Chill the cake pops in refrigerator (for about 15 minutes).

5. Remove the cake pops from the refrigerator. Dip a cake pop into the candy coating. Once completely covered, pull the cake pop out and gently tap the stick on the edge of the bowl to allow the excess candy coating to drip off. Place in a stand.

6. Use the tip of a toothpick to texture the pop all over to create the effect of a wreath. Dip into more candy coating and apply if needed.

7. As the pop hardens, but is still slightly soft, attach the candy cane sprinkles, red sprinkles, and dragées all around the pop.

8. Insert the tip of the white chocolate chip into the center of the pop so the flat base is showing.

9. Tie the red licorice rope into a bow. Dip the tip of a toothpick into green candy coating and dab onto the back of the licorice. Attach the bow above the

chocolate chip, centered on the cake pop. Repeat steps 5 through 9 with remaining cake pops.

10. Let pops stand and dry completely.

DREIDELS

MAKES 24 CAKE POPS

Spin the dreidel. Everybody wins a cake pop!

WHAT YOU'LL NEED

24 uncoated cake dreidels *(shaping instructions below)*
1 14- or 16-oz. bag white candy coating
24 lollipop sticks
Blue edible color pen
Blue sugar sprinkles

WHAT TO DO

1. Prepare the uncoated cake dreidels by first rolling out all of the individual balls for the basic cake pops *(see page 21)*. Then shape each ball into a dreidel by rolling each into a cylinder shape. Gently press the cake against wax paper on the countertop to create four flat sides. Form the tip of the dreidel  with your thumb and forefinger. Place them all on a plate or cookie sheet lined with wax paper.

2. Place the candy coating in a microwave-safe bowl. Melt in the microwave, following the instructions on the package. Stir until you get a smooth consistency.

3. Dip the tip of a lollipop stick into the candy coating about a half inch. Insert dipped end of stick into the bottom of a cake dreidel, making sure it is inserted far enough to achieve stability. Place on a plate or cookie sheet lined with wax paper. Repeat with remaining cake dreidels.

4. Chill the cake pops in refrigerator (for about 15 minutes).

5. Remove the cake pops from the refrigerator. Dip a cake pop into the candy coating. Once completely covered, gently pull the cake pop out and gently tap the stick on the edge of the bowl to allow the excess candy coating to drip off. Place in a stand and let dry completely. Repeat with remaining cake pops.

6. Draw the border lines with the blue edible color pen down all four corners and all the way around on the top and bottom. Draw one symbol on each side: nun, gimel, hay, and shin. Repeat with remaining cake pops.

| NUN | GIMEL | HAY | SHIN |

7. Dip the tip of a toothpick into the white candy coating and gently spread at the base of a pop near the stick. While holding the pop over a bowl, pour the blue sugar sprinkles over the base of the cake pop. Repeat with remaining cake pops.

8. Let pops stand and dry completely.

TIPS

• The lines and detailing for the dreidel can also be done with blue candy coating, using a decorating bag or squeeze bottle.

• To create the basic round cake pops also shown in the photo, follow the instructions on page 21, and tie strands of blue ribbon (about 7" each) around the lollipop sticks.

LOVE BIRDS

MAKES 24 CAKE POPS

A sweet treat for your sweetheart!

WHAT YOU'LL NEED

24 uncoated cake hearts *(shaping instructions below)*
2" heart-shaped cutter
1 14- or 16-oz. bag pink candy coating
24 lollipop sticks
Jumbo daisy sprinkles (optional)
Red edible color pen (optional)
24 jumbo red heart sprinkles
24 candy eyes
24 mini chocolate chips

WHAT TO DO

1. Prepare the uncoated cake hearts by first rolling out all of the individual balls for the basic cake pops *(see page 21)*. Then take a cake ball and press it into the heart-shaped cutter. Set the cutter on a piece of wax paper and flatten the ball inside the  cutter with your fingers. Mold the cake to fit the

heart shape. Then carefully press it out onto the wax paper. Repeat with remaining cake balls.

2. Place the candy coating in a microwave-safe bowl. Melt in the microwave, following the instructions on the package. Stir until you get a smooth consistency.

3. Dip the tip of a lollipop stick into the candy coating about a half inch. Insert dipped end of stick into one of the flat edges of a cake heart. Make sure it is inserted far enough to achieve stability. Place heart on a plate or cookie sheet lined with wax paper. Repeat with remaining cake hearts.

4. Chill the cake pops in refrigerator (for about 15 minutes).

5. If you are using the jumbo daisy sprinkles, use the red edible color pen to dot the center of each one and set them aside.

6. Remove the cake pops from the refrigerator. Dip a cake pop into the candy coating. Once completely covered, pull the cake pop out and gently tap the stick on the edge of the bowl to allow the excess candy coating to drip off. Place in a stand.

7. As the pop begins to harden, but is still slightly soft, attach the jumbo heart sprinkle in the center on the front flat surface of the pop. Then attach the

candy eye, the mini chocolate chip for the nose, and the jumbo daisy sprinkle (if using). Repeat steps 6 and 7 with remaining cake pops.

8. Let stand and dry completely.

TIP

- To create the red heart cake pops that are also shown in the photo, simply dip the cake pops in red candy coating instead of the pink. Then place some melted pink candy coating into a squeeze bottle and pipe the border around the heart.

LEPRECHAUNS AND POTS OF GOLD

These leprechauns and pots of gold are delicious treats at the end of a rainbow!

Leprechauns

MAKES 24 CAKE POPS

WHAT YOU'LL NEED

24 uncoated cake ovals (*shaping instructions on page 94*)
1 14- or 16-oz. bag peach candy coating
24 lollipop sticks
48 Sixlets candies (any color)
48 flat round white sprinkles
Brown edible color pen
Black edible color pen
48 white nonpareil sprinkles
Red edible color pen
Pink edible color pen
1 14- or 16-oz. bag chocolate candy coating
4-oz. squeeze bottle
1 14- or 16-oz. bag green candy coating
1-1/2" round mint candy mold
24 Rolo caramel candies
Food-safe paintbrush
3g gold pearl dust
24 strands of green ribbon (about 7" each)

WHAT TO DO

1. Prepare the uncoated cake ovals by first rolling out all of the individual balls for the basic cake pops *(see page 21)*. Then shape each ball into an oval by gently squeezing in one hand turning slightly, to create the oval. Round each top, and lightly pinch the bottom for the chin. Place them all on a plate or cookie sheet lined with wax paper.

2. Place the peach candy coating in a microwave-safe bowl. Melt in the microwave, following the instructions on the package. Stir until you get a smooth consistency.

3. Dip the tip of a lollipop stick into the peach candy coating about a half inch. Insert dipped end of stick into the bottom of a cake oval, making sure it is inserted far enough to achieve stability. Place oval on a plate or cookie sheet lined with wax paper. Repeat with remaining cake ovals.

4. Chill the cake pops in refrigerator (for about 15 minutes).

5. Remove the cake pops from the refrigerator. Place two of the Sixlets candies on the front of a pop, positioning them for the cheeks. Gently press against the uncoated pop so that they stay on their own. Repeat with remaining cake pops.

6. Dip the cake pop—with the Sixlets firmly in place—into the peach candy coating. Once completely covered, gently pull the cake pop out and gently tap the stick on the edge of the bowl to allow the excess candy coating to drip off. Place in a stand and let dry completely. Repeat with remaining cake pops.

7. Create the eyes: Place the flat white sprinkles on wax paper. Draw a circle with the brown edible color pen covering most of the white sprinkle, leaving a crescent moon shape of the white still showing. In the bottom corner of the brown circle, draw a smaller circle with the black edible color pen. Dip the tip of a toothpick into the peach candy coating and dab onto the black circle, and attach a white nonpareil. Repeat this process to create all 48 eyes.

8. With the end of a toothpick or extra lollipop stick, dab a small amount of peach candy coating onto the cake pop where the eyes will be positioned. Attach each of the eyes. Repeat with remaining cake pops.

9. Dip the end of a lollipop stick into the peach candy coating. Dab onto the front of the cake pop in between the cheeks to create the nose. Let dry. Repeat with remaining cake pops.

10. Draw on the mouth with the red edible color pen. Draw on the eyelashes and eyebrows with the brown edible color pen. Lightly brush the pink edible color pen over the cheeks to give them a rosy glow. Dip the tip of a toothpick into the peach candy coating. Dab onto the side of the pop to create the ears. Repeat with remaining cake pops.

11. Place the chocolate candy coating in a microwave-safe bowl. Melt in the microwave, following the instructions on the package. Stir until you get a smooth consistency.

12. Fill the squeeze bottle with the chocolate candy coating. Pipe on the hair, starting in the center on the top. Pipe down the side until the chocolate reaches the top of the ear. Repeat with remaining cake pops.

13. Place the green candy coating in a microwave-safe bowl. Melt in the microwave, following the instruc-

tions on the package. Stir until you get a smooth consistency.

14. Create the hat: Fill the round mint candy mold with the green candy coating. Let sit until completely hardened. Remove each disc from the candy mold and set aside. (You'll need 24 discs in total.) Place the narrow end of a Rolo on the end of a toothpick and dip into the green candy coating. Once completely covered, gently pull the Rolo out and gently tap the toothpick on the edge of the bowl to allow the excess candy coating to drip off. Place in a Styrofoam stand and let dry completely. Once hardened, carefully remove the toothpick and set in the center of the round green disc, attaching with green candy coating. Dip a small food-safe paintbrush into the gold pearl dust and brush all the way around the base of the Rolo candy to create a gold band on the hat. Repeat this process to create all 24 hats.

15. Pipe a small amount of chocolate candy coating on top of the pop, over the hair, and attach the hat. Repeat with remaining cake pops.

16. Tie a ribbon around the lollipop stick at the base of the head, and repeat with remaining cake pops.

17. Let pops stand and dry completely.

POTS OF GOLD

MAKES 24 CAKE POPS

WHAT YOU'LL NEED

24 uncoated round cake balls
1 14- or 16-oz. bag black candy coating
24 lollipop sticks
3 oz. gold pearlized sugar crystals
24 strands of rainbow ribbon (about 7" each)

WHAT TO DO

1. Prepare the uncoated round cake balls *(see basic pop recipe on page 21).*

2. Place the candy coating in a microwave-safe bowl. Melt in the microwave, following the instructions on the package. Stir until you get a smooth consistency.

3. Dip the tip of a lollipop stick into the candy coating about a half inch. Insert dipped end of stick into a cake ball, about halfway through the ball. Place ball on a plate or cookie sheet lined with wax paper. Repeat with remaining cake balls.

4. Chill the cake pops in refrigerator (for about 15 minutes).

5. Remove the cake pops from the refrigerator. Dip a cake pop into the candy coating. Once completely

covered, pull the cake pop out and gently tap the stick on the edge of the bowl to allow the excess candy coating to drip off. Place upside down on wax paper and gently press the cake pop to create a flat surface and a slight brim for the pot. Let dry completely. Repeat with remaining cake pops.

6. Once the pops have hardened, gently peel them away from the wax paper and place them in a stand.

7. Spoon a small amount of candy coating onto the flat surface of the cake pop. Sprinkle the gold pearlized sugar crystals all over to create a mound of "gold." Repeat with remaining cake pops.

8. Tie a ribbon around the lollipop stick at the base of the pot, and repeat with remaining cake pops.

9. Let pops stand and dry completely.

TIP

- Instead of using a regular lollipop stick, try using a multi-colored candy cane instead!

EASTER BUNNIES

These bunnies are almost too cute to eat!

WHAT YOU'LL NEED

24 uncoated round cake balls
1 14- or 16-oz. bag white candy coating
24 lollipop sticks
48 candy corn
48 candy eyes
24 pink round confetti sprinkles
48 green candy-coated chocolate sunflower seeds
Black edible color pen
48 white nonpareil sprinkles
48 jumbo daisy sprinkles
48 mini yellow sprinkles
Food-safe paintbrush
Pink sparkle dust

WHAT TO DO

1. Prepare the uncoated round cake balls *(see basic pop recipe on page 21)*.

2. Place the candy coating in a microwave-safe bowl. Melt in the microwave, following the instructions on the package. Stir until you get a smooth consistency.

3. Dip the tip of a lollipop stick into the candy coating about a half inch. Insert dipped end of stick into a cake ball, about halfway through the ball. Place ball on a plate or cookie sheet lined with wax paper. Repeat with remaining cake balls.

4. Chill the cake pops in refrigerator (for about 15 minutes).

5. Remove the cake pops from the refrigerator. Dip the tip of a candy corn into the white candy coating. Stick the tip into the top of the cake pop slightly off center, for one of the ears. Repeat for the other ear and let both harden. Repeat with remaining cake pops.

6. Dip the cake pop—with the candy corn firmly in place—into the white candy coating. Once completely covered, pull the cake pop out and gently

tap the stick on the edge of the bowl to allow the excess candy coating to drip off. Place in a stand.

7. As the pop begins to harden, but is still slightly soft, attach the candy eyes and pink sprinkle for the nose. In front of one of the ears, place two sunflower seeds so the rounded ends touch. Repeat steps 6 and 7 with remaining cake pops.

8. After the pops have hardened, draw the mouth on each of the pops with the black edible color pen.

9. Dip the tip of a toothpick into the white candy coating and dab it onto the end points of the smile. Then place a white nonpareil at each end. Dip the toothpick again and dab some candy coating onto the point where the sunflower seeds meet. Attach the flower sprinkle. Use more candy coating to attach a yellow sprinkle to the center of the flower. Repeat with remaining cake pops.

10. Dip a small, food-safe paintbrush into the pink sparkle dust. Lightly brush onto the cheeks and the front of both ears. Repeat steps with remaining cake pops.

11. Let pops stand and dry completely.

HATCHING CHICKS

MAKES 24 CAKE POPS

Watch as these lovable baby chicks hatch their way into your Easter festivities.

WHAT YOU'LL NEED

24 uncoated cake ovals *(shaping instructions below)*
1 14- or 16-oz. bag yellow candy coating
24 lollipop sticks
1 14- or 16-oz. bag white candy coating
4-oz. squeeze bottle
48 mini yellow candy-coated chocolate candy
24 orange crunch sprinkles
Black edible color pen

WHAT TO DO

1. Prepare the uncoated cake ovals by first rolling out all of the individual balls for the basic cake pops *(see page 21)*. Then shape each ball into an oval by gently squeezing in one hand and turning slightly, to create the oval. Place them all on a plate  or cookie sheet lined with wax paper.

2. Place the yellow candy coating in a microwave-safe bowl. Melt in the microwave, following the instructions on the package. Stir until you get a smooth consistency.

3. Dip the tip of a lollipop stick into the candy coating about a half inch. Insert dipped end of stick into the wide base of the cake oval, making sure it is inserted far enough to achieve stability. Place oval on a plate or cookie sheet lined with wax paper. Repeat with remaining cake ovals.

4. Chill the cake pops in refrigerator (for about 15 minutes).

5. Remove the cake pops from the refrigerator. Dip the cake pop into the yellow candy coating. Once completely covered, pull the cake pop out and gently tap the stick on the edge of the bowl to allow the excess candy coating to drip off. Place in a stand and let dry completely. Repeat with remaining cake pops.

6. Place the white candy coating in a microwave-safe bowl. Melt in the microwave, following the instructions on the package. Stir until you get a smooth consistency.

7. Fill the squeeze bottle with the white candy coating. On the bottom third of a pop, pipe on the candy coating to create the broken edges first. Go

all the way around. Once you have established the lines for the broken shell, fill in the rest below to create the base of the shell. Complete this part while holding the pop over a bowl and let the excess drip off. Place in a stand and let dry completely. Repeat with remaining cake pops.

8. Carefully, pipe onto the top of a cake pop creating the top portion of the broken egg shell. Make sure the candy coating has hardened a little, so that it doesn't drip down the sides. Let stand and dry completely. Repeat with remaining cake pops.

9. Dip the tip of a toothpick into the yellow candy coating and dab it onto a pop where the wings and beak will be positioned. Gently attach the yellow candy-coated chocolate candies for the wings and orange crunch sprinkle for the beak.

10. Draw on the eyes with the black edible color pen. Repeat steps 9 and 10 with remaining cake pops.

11. Let pops stand and dry completely.

BiRTHDAYS
& BABiES

· · · · · · · · · · · ·

Take your birthday parties and baby
showers to the next level! Cake pops
are the next best thing to (if not better than) regular cake. So, give your
party guests something to smile
about at the next big celebration!

Have a blast with colorful **Clowns** or
gorgeous **Garden Fairies**. Monkey
around with playful **Monkeys** and
dangerous **Dinosaurs**. Or put a
modern twist on an old-fashioned
favorite with **Milkshake** cake pops.
Try the cuddly **Teddy Bears** or cute
little **Baby Feet** for a baby shower,
and welcome the newest additions to
the world with treats almost as cute
as the little ones themselves!

CLOWNS

MAKES 24 CAKE POPS

*You'll want to clown around with these cake pops—
guaranteed to make you smile!*

WHAT YOU'LL NEED

24 uncoated round cake balls
1 14- or 16-oz. bag white candy coating
48 lollipop sticks (24 for the cake pops, 24 for creating the hats)
1 14- or 16-oz. bag peach candy coating (optional)
24 mini red M&M's
48 candy eyes
48 diamond-shaped sprinkles
Red edible color pen
48 round confetti sprinkles
1 14- or 16-oz. bag lavender candy coating (optional)
24 sugar ice-cream cones
Rainbow nonpareils (optional)
1 package of Nerd Rope Candy
48 mini baking cups (24 polka dot, 24 solid color)

WHAT TO DO

1. Prepare the uncoated round cake balls *(see basic pop recipe on page 21)*.

2. Place the white candy coating in a microwave-safe bowl. Melt in the microwave, following the instruc-

tions on the package. Stir until you get a smooth consistency.

3. Dip the tip of a lollipop stick into the white candy coating about a half inch. Insert dipped end of stick into a cake ball, about halfway through the ball. Place ball on a plate or cookie sheet lined with wax paper. Repeat with remaining cake balls.

4. Chill the cake pops in refrigerator (for about 15 minutes).

5. Remove the cake pops from the refrigerator. Dip a cake pop into the white candy coating. Once completely covered, pull the cake pop out and gently tap the stick on the edge of the bowl to allow the excess candy coating to drip off. Place in a stand and let dry completely. Repeat with remaining cake pops.

6. To create a clown with a 2-toned painted face: Place the peach candy coating in a microwave-safe bowl. Melt in the microwave, following the instructions on the package. Stir until you get a smooth consistency. Dip a cake pop into the peach candy coating twice at altering 45° angles, leaving the white portion still showing at the bottom of the pop. Place in a stand and let dry completely. Repeat with remaining cake pops.

7. Dip the tip of a toothpick in the peach* candy coating and dab a small amount in the center on the front of the cake pop where the nose will be positioned. Attach the mini red M&M for the nose. Using more candy coating as glue, attach the candy eyes and diamond-shaped sprinkles for the eyebrows.

8. Draw on the mouth with the red edible color pen. Dip the tip of a toothpick in the peach* candy coating and dab a small amount for the cheeks and attach the round confetti sprinkles. Repeat steps 7 and 8 with remaining cake pops.

9. Place the lavender candy coating in a microwave-safe bowl. Melt in the microwave, following the instructions on the package. Stir until you get a smooth consistency.

10. Create the hats: Cut off the bottom 2 inches of each of the sugar ice-cream cones. Dip the tip of a lollipop stick into the lavender candy coating and place in a stand. Immediately after, place the 2" piece of one of the cones over the stick and let harden against the candy coating. Once secure, remove the stick from the stand, and dip the ice-cream cone into the lavender candy coating. Once completely covered, pull the ice-cream cone out and gently tap the stick on the edge of the bowl to allow the excess candy coating to drip off. Place

back in the stand and cover with the rainbow non-pareils. Let dry completely. Repeat this process to create all 24 ice-cream cone hats.

11. Dip the tip of a toothpick in the peach* candy coating and dab a small amount on the top of a cake pop. Gently remove the ice-cream cone hat from the lollipop stick and attach on top of the pop. Hold until it hardens and stays on its own. Repeat with remaining cake pops.

12. Cut the Nerd Rope Candy into 1/2" pieces. Dip the tip of a toothpick in the peach* candy coating and dab onto either side of the cake pop, just below the hat, where the hair will be positioned. Attach the candy pieces on the pop to create the hair on each side. Repeat with remaining cake pops.

13. Poke a small hole in the center of each of the mini baking cups with a pair of scissors, or other sharp object. Take one polka-dot cup and insert the lollipop stick through the hole, sliding the cup all the way up to the base of the clown's head. Then repeat with a solid-colored cup and position it underneath the polka dot cup. Repeat with remaining cake pops.

14. Let stand and dry completely.

TIPS

• If you don't want to use baking cups for the collars, you could easily substitute bows.

• The hats don't have to be dipped in candy melt. They'd also look good as plain ice-cream cones on top.

If you are not creating the 2-toned painted faces, then use white candy coating instead of peach when it's referenced in steps 7, 8, 11, and 12.

DINOSAURS

MAKES 24 CAKE POPS

*It won't be long before these dinosaur cake pops
go extinct at your next party!*

WHAT YOU'LL NEED

24 uncoated cake dinosaur heads *(shaping instructions
  below)*
1 14- or 16-oz. bag green candy coating
1 14- or 16-oz. bag orange candy coating
24 lollipop sticks
Heart-shaped sprinkles (white, blue, orange, yellow)
48 candy eyes
Black edible color pen

WHAT TO DO

1. Prepare the uncoated cake
    dinosaur heads by first
    rolling out all of the indi-
    vidual balls for the basic
    cake pops *(see page 21)*.
    Then place each ball on
    wax paper on the kitchen
    counter and press down
    across the center of the ball
    using the side of your fin-
    ger. This will help create the shape for the nose and

will shift some of the cake to the back. Shape the back of the ball so it raises up a little higher. Gently press your thumb and forefinger in the center to create the position for the eyes. Repeat with remaining cake balls and place all the dinosaur heads on a plate or cookie sheet lined with wax paper.

2. Place the green and orange candy coating in separate microwave-safe bowls. Melt in the microwave, following the instructions on the package. Stir until you get a smooth consistency.

3. Dip the tip of a lollipop stick into either the green or orange candy coating about a half inch. Insert dipped end of stick into the bottom of the cake dinosaur head, making sure it is inserted far enough to achieve stability. Place dinosaur head on a plate or cookie sheet lined with wax paper. Repeat with remaining cake dinosaur heads.

4. Chill the cake pops in refrigerator (for about 15 minutes).

5. Remove the cake pops from the refrigerator. In this recipe I am suggesting you create 12 green and 12 orange dinosaur cake pops. Although, you could do all the same color if you'd like. Dip a cake pop into the green candy coating. Once completely covered, gently pull the cake pop out and gently tap the stick on the edge of the bowl to allow the excess candy coating to

drip off. Place in a stand. Repeat for 11 more of the cake pops. Then repeat the same process with the orange candy coating with the remaining 12 cake pops.

6. As the candy coating hardens, but is still slightly soft, attach the candy hearts for the spikes on the top of the head. Lay one heart flat, slightly above where the eyes will go. Line four hearts in a row behind that, sticking the rounded end into the cake pop so the pointed ends are sticking up.

7. Next, attach three or four white candy hearts for the teeth. Stick the rounded end of the hearts into the pop so only the pointed ends are exposed. Line these on the front of the pop across the lower the portion.

8. Dip the tip of a toothpick in the green or orange candy coating and dab a small amount in the indented sections where the eyes will be positioned. Attach the candy eyes. Repeat steps 6 through 8 with remaining cake pops.

9. Draw dots on the nose for the nostrils with the black edible color pen. Repeat with remaining cake pops.

10. Let pops stand and dry completely.

TIP

• Feel free to mix and match the dinosaur spikes to create fun color combinations!

GARDEN FAIRIES

These cute fluttering fairies will be the highlight of any little girl's party!

WHAT YOU'LL NEED

24 uncoated cake fairy bodies *(shaping instructions below)*
1 14- or 16-oz. bag pink candy coating
24 lollipop sticks
1 14- or 16-oz. bag peach candy coating
Large handful of milk chocolate candy coating wafers
24 regular-sized pink flower sprinkles
Black edible color pen
Red edible color pen
4-oz. squeeze bottle
24 jumbo white flower sprinkles
24 silk flowers

WHAT TO DO

1. Prepare the uncoated cake fairy bodies by first rolling out all of the individual balls for the basic cake pops *(see page 21)*. Then shape each ball into a fairy body by taking one-third of the original ball, and creating a smaller ball about 1 inch in diameter. This will be the head. Gently squeeze the remaining portion of the original ball between your fingers.

Taper at the base, widening out in the middle, and then tapering back at the top. Flatten the top with your fingers. This will be the body. Repeat with remaining cake balls and place all the components on a plate or cookie sheet lined with wax paper.

2. Place the pink candy coating in a microwave-safe bowl. Melt in the microwave, following the instructions on the package. Stir until you get a smooth consistency.

3. Dip the tip of a lollipop stick into the pink candy coating about a half inch. Insert dipped end of stick into the bottom of a cake body shape, making sure it is inserted far enough to achieve stability. Dip the tip of a toothpick into the candy coating and brush on the top of the cake body shape. Attach a head by placing a small ball on top and hold until it stays

on its own. Place fairy body on a plate or cookie sheet lined with wax paper. Repeat with remaining cake shapes to assemble the rest of the fairy bodies.

4. Chill the cake pops in refrigerator (for about 15 minutes).

5. Remove the cake pops from the refrigerator. Dip a cake pop into the pink candy coating. Once completely covered, gently pull the cake pop out and gently tap the stick on the edge of the bowl to allow the excess candy coating to drip off. Place in a stand and let dry completely. Repeat with remaining cake pops.

6. Place the peach and milk chocolate candy coating in separate microwave-safe bowls. Melt in the microwave, following the instructions on the package. Stir until you get a smooth consistency.

7. Dip the top of a cake pop into the peach candy coating, only covering the head. Hold upside down until all of the excess drips back into the bowl. Place in a stand and let dry completely. Repeat with remaining cake pops.

8. Dip the tip of a toothpick in the melted chocolate and texturize the top of a cake pop to create the hair. Dab the toothpick onto the top of the pop and drag downward in small, short motions.

9. As the chocolate hardens, but is still slightly soft, place the regular-sized pink flower sprinkle in the hair. Repeat steps 8 and 9 with remaining cake pops.

10. Dip the tip of a toothpick in the peach candy coating and dab a small amount in the center of the face for the nose. Draw on the eyes and mouth with the black and red edible color pens. Repeat with remaining cake pops.

11. Fill the squeeze bottle with the peach candy coating. Pipe on the arms, starting on one side of the pop at the base of the neck, and curving it down across the center of the body stopping in the middle of the stomach. Repeat on the opposite side for the other arm. Attach the jumbo white flower sprinkle in the middle where the arms meet. Dip the tip of a toothpick in the pink candy coating and dab in the center of the flower. Let stand and dry completely. Repeat with remaining cake pops.

12. Create the skirt: Disassemble a silk flower. For each skirt you will need the bottom two or three layers of petals of the flower. Poke a small hole near the narrow end of each petal with a pair of scissors or other sharp object. Take one petal and insert the lollipop stick through the hole, sliding the petal all the way up to the base of the fairy's body. Repeat

with remaining petals. Then repeat with remaining cake pops.

TIPS

- The skirt can be made from most any kind of artificial flower of any color.

- To create the flower cake pops also shown in the photo, follow the instructions for the basic cake pops on page 21. Then follow the same instructions in step 12 to assemble the flower petals around the basic cake pop.

MILKSHAKES

MAKES 24 CAKE POPS

Milkshake cake pops will bring back a bit of nostalgia with every enjoyable bite.

WHAT YOU'LL NEED

24 uncoated cake cones *(shaping instructions below)*
1 14- or 16-oz. bag milk chocolate candy coating
24 lollipop sticks
1 decorating bag
1 #18 decorating tip
16-oz. container store-bought vanilla frosting
24 red chocolate crunch sprinkles
24 pieces of red licorice rope (cut to about 1-1/2" each)

WHAT TO DO

1. Prepare the uncoated cake cones by first rolling out all of the individual balls for the basic cake pops *(see page 21)*. Then shape each ball into a cone by gently squeezing each ball between your fingers. Taper the ball at one end and create a wider base at the other

end. Flatten the top of the shape with your fingers or against wax paper placed on the kitchen counter. Place them all on a plate or cookie sheet lined with wax paper.

2. Place the candy coating in a microwave-safe bowl. Melt in the microwave, following the instructions on the package. Stir until you get a smooth consistency.

3. Dip the tip of a lollipop stick into the candy coating about a half inch. Insert dipped end of stick into the bottom of a cake cone, making sure it is inserted far enough to achieve stability. Place cake cone on a plate or cookie sheet lined with wax paper. Repeat with remaining cake cones.

4. Chill the cake pops in refrigerator (for about 15 minutes).

5. Remove the cake pops from the refrigerator. Dip a cake pop into the candy coating. Once completely covered, gently pull the cake pop out and gently tap the stick on the edge of the bowl to allow the excess candy coating to drip off. Place in a stand and let dry completely. Repeat with remaining cake pops.

6. Attach the #18 tip to the decorating bag. Fill the decorating bag with vanilla frosting. Pipe frosting onto the top of a cake pop in a circular motion,

creating the effect of whipped cream. Repeat with remaining cake pops.

7. Place the red chocolate crunch sprinkle on top of the frosting.

8. Insert the licorice rope piece into the frosting at an angle to make a straw. Make sure it is secure enough to stay on its own and bend the end of the straw slightly. Repeat steps 7 and 8 with remaining cake pops.

9. Let pops stand and dry completely.

MONKEYS

MAKES 24 CAKE POPS

*These delightful cake pops will have
everyone monkeying around!*

WHAT YOU'LL NEED

24 uncoated cake monkey heads *(shaping instructions
   below)*
1 14- or 16-oz. bag milk chocolate candy coating
24 lollipop sticks
48 chocolate chips
Small handful of white candy coating wafers
4-oz. squeeze bottle
48 candy eyes
Black edible color pen
24 pieces of brown pipe cleaner (about 5" each)
   (optional)
24 Banana Runts candy (optional)

WHAT TO DO

1. Prepare the uncoated cake monkey heads by first
   rolling out all of the individual balls for the basic
   cake pops *(see page 21)*. Then place each ball on
   wax paper on the kitchen counter and press down
   across the center of the ball using the side of your
   finger to create a slight ridge. Pick up the cake ball
   and gently round it with your fingers. Repeat with

remaining cake balls and place all the monkey heads on a plate or cookie sheet lined with wax paper.

2. Place the milk chocolate candy coating in a microwave-safe bowl. Melt in the microwave, following the instructions on the package. Stir until you get a smooth consistency.

3. Dip the tip of a lollipop stick into the milk chocolate candy coating about a half inch. Insert dipped end of stick into the bottom of a cake monkey head, making sure it is inserted far enough to achieve stability. Place monkey head on a plate or cookie sheet lined with wax paper. Repeat with remaining cake monkey heads.

4. Chill the cake pops in refrigerator (for about 15 minutes).

5. Remove the cake pops from the refrigerator. Dip the tip of a toothpick into the melted chocolate and dab onto the sides of the cake pop toward the top where you will position the ears. Gently press the chocolate chips against the melted chocolate with the flat surface facing forward. Hold until they set and stay on their own. Repeat with remaining cake pops.

6. Dip a cake pop—with the chocolate chips firmly attached—into the chocolate candy coating. Once completely covered, pull the cake pop out and gently tap the stick on the edge of the bowl to allow the excess candy coating to drip off. Place in a stand and let dry completely. Repeat with remaining cake pops.

7. Add the small handful of white candy coating wafers to the remaining melted chocolate. Melt in the microwave. Stir until you get a smooth consistency. This will create a light brown color.

8. Fill the squeeze bottle with the light brown chocolate. Pipe onto the front of a cake pop, creating the outline for the face first, then filling it in. Gently tap the stick against the palm of your hand to smooth out the face. Dab a dot of chocolate onto

each of the ears. Place in a stand and let dry completely. Repeat with remaining cake pops.

9. Dip the tip of a toothpick into the melted chocolate. Dab on the front of the cake pop where the eyes will be positioned and attach the candy eyes.

10. Draw the mouth, nose, and eyebrows with the black edible color pen. Repeat steps 9 and 10 with remaining cake pops.

11. Let pops stand and dry completely.

12. If you want to create the monkey arms, twist the center of the pipe cleaner around a stick and curl the arms. Slide to the top so it sits beneath the cake ball. Curl the end of one of the arms around a piece of Banana Runts candy. Repeat with remaining cake pops.

TIPS

• When creating the ears, it's important to attach the chocolate chips to the cake ball using the melted chocolate as the glue. Otherwise they may fall off.

• M&M's can also be used to create the ears.

POLAR BEARS

MAKES 24 CAKE POPS

Polar bears might come from a cold climate, but these cake pops are guaranteed to warm your heart!

WHAT YOU'LL NEED

24 uncoated cake bear heads *(shaping instructions below)*
1 14- or 16-oz. bag white candy coating
24 lollipop sticks
48 M&M's (any color)
Black edible color pen

WHAT TO DO

1. Prepare the uncoated cake bear heads by first rolling out all of the individual balls for the basic cake pops *(see page 21).* Then shape each ball into a bear head by first placing a ball in the palm of your hand. Squeeze the top of the ball with the thumb and forefinger of your other hand to create a pointed nose. Smooth

out the nose and round the rest of the cake pop with your fingers. Place them all on a plate or cookie sheet lined with wax paper.

2. Place the candy coating in a microwave-safe bowl. Melt in the microwave, following the instructions on the package. Stir until you get a smooth consistency.

3. Dip the tip of a lollipop stick into the candy coating about a half inch. Insert dipped end of stick into the bottom of the cake bear head, making sure it is inserted far enough to achieve stability. Place bear head on a plate or cookie sheet lined with wax paper. Repeat with remaining cake bear heads.

4. Chill the cake pops in refrigerator (for about 15 minutes).

5. Remove the cake pops from the refrigerator. Press 2 M&M's (one on each side) of a cake pop toward the top to create an indent where the ears will be positioned. Dip the tip of a toothpick into the candy coating and dab in the two indents. Gently press the M&M's against the candy coating and hold until they are secure and stay on their own. Repeat with remaining cake pops.

6. Dip a cake pop—with the M&M's firmly attached—into the candy coating. Once completely covered, pull the cake pop out and gently tap the

stick on the edge of the bowl to allow the excess candy coating to drip off. Place in a stand and let dry completely. Repeat with remaining cake pops.

7. With the black edible color pen, draw the eyes, nose, and mouth onto a cake pop. Dot the cheeks and fill in the ears. Repeat with remaining cake pops.

8. Let pops stand and dry completely.

TIP

• For added pizzazz, bundle up your polar bear by tying some ribbon around the stick to look like a winter scarf.

BABY FEET

MAKES 24 CAKE POPS

Cake pops so cute they'll make you want to tickle these toes before you eat them!

WHAT YOU'LL NEED

24 uncoated round cake balls
1 14- or 16-oz. bag white candy coating
24 lollipop sticks
1 14- or 16-oz. bag blue candy coating
1 14- or 16-oz. bag pink candy coating
2 decorating bags
2 #2 decorating tips

WHAT TO DO

1. Prepare the uncoated round cake balls *(see basic pop recipe on page 21)*.

2. Place the white candy coating in a microwave-safe bowl. Melt in the microwave, following the instructions on the package. Stir until you get a smooth consistency.

3. Dip the tip of a lollipop stick into the white candy coating about a half inch. Insert dipped end of stick into a cake ball, about halfway through the ball. Place ball on a plate or cookie sheet lined with wax paper. Repeat with remaining cake balls.

4. Chill the cake pops in refrigerator (for about 15 minutes).

5. Remove the cake pops from the refrigerator. Dip a cake pop into the white candy coating. Once completely covered, pull the cake pop out and gently tap the stick on the edge of the bowl to allow the excess candy coating to drip off. Place in a stand and let dry completely. Repeat with remaining cake pops.

6. In this recipe I am suggesting you create 12 blue and 12 pink baby feet cake pops. Although you could do all the same color if you'd like. Place the blue and pink candy coating into separate microwave-safe bowls. Melt in the microwave, following the instructions on the package. Stir until you get a smooth consistency.

7. Attach the #2 tips to separate decorating bags. Fill one decorating bag with the blue candy coating and fill the other with the pink candy coating.

8. On top of a cake pop, pipe the blue candy coating outline for the first foot, and then fill in. Make sure you leave enough room to make two feet on top of the cake pop. Gently tap the end of the lollipop stick against the counter to smooth out the foot. Dab on dots for the toes. Repeat for the second foot. Place in a stand. Repeat for 11 more of the

cake pops. Then repeat the same process with the pink candy coating for the remaining 12 cake pops.

9. Let pops stand and dry completely.

TIPS

- To create the basic cake pops also pictured in the photo, follow the instructions on page 21.

TEDDY BEARS

*Make that special baby shower super sweet
with these adorable teddy bear pops!*

WHAT YOU'LL NEED

24 uncoated cake bear heads *(shaping instructions
  below)*
1 14- or 16-oz. bag milk chocolate candy coating
24 lollipop sticks
48 M&M's (any color)
Small handful of dark chocolate candy coating wafers
1 decorating bag
#2 decorating tip
24 strands of pink and blue ribbon (about 7" each)

WHAT TO DO

1. Prepare the uncoated cake bear heads by first
   rolling out all of the individual balls for the basic
   cake pops *(see page 21)*. Then shape each ball into
   a bear head by first placing a ball in the palm of
   your hand. Squeeze the top of the ball with the
   thumb and forefinger of your other hand to create
   a pointed nose. Smooth out the nose and round
   the rest of the cake pop with your fingers. Place
   them all on a plate or cookie sheet lined with wax
   paper.

2. Place the milk chocolate candy coating in a microwave-safe bowl. Melt in the microwave, following the instructions on the package. Stir until you get a smooth consistency.

3. Dip the tip of a lollipop stick into the milk chocolate candy coating about a half inch. Insert dipped end of stick into the bottom of a cake bear head, making sure it is inserted far enough to achieve stability. Place bear head on a plate or cookie sheet lined with wax paper. Repeat with remaining cake bear heads.

4. Chill the cake pops in refrigerator (for about 15 minutes).

5. Remove the cake pops from the refrigerator. Press 2 M&M's (one on each side) of a cake pop toward

the top to create an indent where the ears will be positioned. Dip the tip of a toothpick into the candy coating and dab in the two indents. Gently press the M&M's against the candy coating and hold until they are secure and stay on their own. Repeat with remaining cake pops.

6. Dip the cake pop—with the M&M's firmly attached—into the milk chocolate candy coating. Once completely covered, pull the cake pop out and gently tap the stick on the edge of the bowl to allow the excess candy coating to drip off. Place in a stand and let dry. Repeat with remaining cake pops.

7. Dip the tip of a toothpick into the milk chocolate candy coating and dab the toothpick against the cake pop and lift up quickly to create the "fur" texture. Repeat this motion until the face is completely covered, but make sure to leave the front of the ears smooth. Let stand and dry completely. Repeat with remaining cake pops.

8. Place the dark chocolate candy coating into a microwave-safe bowl. Melt in the microwave. Stir until you get a smooth consistency.

9. Attach the #2 decorating tip to the decorating bag and fill the bag with the melted dark chocolate. Pipe the eyes, nose, and mouth onto a cake pop. Repeat with remaining cake pops.

10. Tie a ribbon around the lollipop stick at the base of the head, and repeat with remaining cake pops.

11. Let pops stand and dry completely.

SUN & FUN
ALL-OCCASION

• • • • • • • • • • • • •

Cake pops are perfect for any and all occasions. Plan your next party around a themed cake pop and coordinate the accent pieces to match this delicious treat. They'll be everyone's favorite party favor and will quickly become the focal point of the dessert table.

It's game time whenever the **Sports Balls** are in play. Or kick back, relax, and enjoy some fun in the sun with the **Beach** cake pops. And, you'll love nibbling on a **Piña Colada** cake pop while you're sipping on the real thing.

SPORTS BALLS

(FOOTBALLS, BASEBALLS, BASKETBALLS, & SOCCER BALLS)

These cake pops will score big with your crowd!

FOOTBALLS

MAKES 24 CAKE POPS

WHAT YOU'LL NEED

24 uncoated cake footballs *(shaping instructions below)*
1 14- or 16-oz. bag milk chocolate candy coating
24 lollipop sticks
Large handful of white candy coating wafers
1 decorating bag
1 #1 decorating tip

WHAT TO DO

1. Prepare the uncoated cake footballs by first rolling out all of the individual balls for the basic cake pops *(see page 21)*. Then begin to shape each one into an oval by gently squeezing in  one hand and turning slightly to create the oval. Gently pinch the ends until they are somewhat

pointed. Smooth out the rest of the cake pop with your fingers. Place them all on a plate or cookie sheet lined with wax paper.

2. Place the milk chocolate candy coating in a microwave-safe bowl. Melt in the microwave, following the instructions on the package. Stir until you get a smooth consistency.

3. Dip the tip of a lollipop stick into the milk chocolate candy coating about a half inch. Insert dipped end of stick into the bottom of a cake football, making sure it is inserted far enough to achieve stability. Place football on a plate or cookie sheet lined with wax paper. Repeat with remaining cake footballs.

4. Chill the cake pops in refrigerator (for about 15 minutes).

5. Remove the cake pops from the refrigerator. Dip a cake pop into the milk chocolate candy coating. Once completely covered, gently pull the cake pop out and gently tap the stick on the edge of the bowl to allow the excess candy coating to drip off. Place in a stand and let dry completely. Repeat with remaining cake pops.

6. Place the white candy coating into a microwave-safe bowl. Melt in the microwave, following the instructions on the package. Stir until you get a smooth consistency.

7. Attach the #1 decorating tip to the decorating bag and fill the bag with the white candy coating. Pipe the lines onto each of the footballs.

8. Let pops stand and dry completely.

TIP

• Footballs are also fun to make in coordinating colors with your favorite team. Or mix it up by piping on the number of your favorite player.

Baseballs, Basketballs, & Soccer Balls

MAKES 24 CAKE POPS

What You'll Need

24 uncoated round cake balls
1 14- or 16-oz. bag white candy coating
1 14- or 16-oz. bag orange candy coating
24 lollipop sticks
Black edible color pen
Red edible color pen

What To Do

1. Prepare the uncoated round cake balls *(see basic pop recipe on page 21)*.

2. Place the white and orange candy coating into separate microwave-safe bowls. Melt in the microwave, following the instructions on the package. Stir until you get a smooth consistency.

3. In this recipe I am suggesting you create 8 baseball, 8 basketball, and 8 soccer ball cake pops, though of course you could do all the same or any variety that you'd like. Dip the tip of a lollipop stick into the white or orange candy coating about a half inch. Insert dipped end of stick into a cake ball, about halfway through the ball. Place ball on a

plate or cookie sheet lined with wax paper. Repeat with remaining cake balls.

4. Chill the cake pops in refrigerator (for about 15 minutes).

5. Remove the cake pops from the refrigerator. Dip a cake pop into the white or orange candy coating. Once completely covered, pull the cake pop out and gently tap the stick on the edge of the bowl to allow the excess candy coating to drip off. Place in a stand and let dry completely. Repeat with remaining cake pops.

6. Use the black edible color pen to draw the lines for each of the soccer and basketball cake pops. Use the red edible color pen to draw the seams for the baseball cake pops.

7. Let pops stand and dry completely.

MINIATURE GOLF

MAKES 24 CAKE POPS

These mini golf cake pops are a hole in one!

WHAT YOU'LL NEED

24 uncoated round cake balls
1 14- or 16-oz. bag green candy coating
24 lollipop sticks
Green sugar sprinkles
Black edible color pen
24 green candy coating wafers (reserve for putting green decoration)
24 white dragée sprinkles
2 pieces of red 8-1/2" x 11" cardstock paper
24 toothpicks

WHAT TO DO

1. Prepare the uncoated round cake balls *(see basic pop recipe on page 21).*

2. Place the bag of candy coating in a microwave-safe bowl. Melt in the microwave, following the instructions on the package. Stir until you get a smooth consistency.

3. Dip the tip of a lollipop stick into the candy coating about a half inch. Insert dipped end of stick into a cake ball, about halfway through the ball.

Place ball on a plate or cookie sheet lined with wax paper. Repeat with remaining cake balls.

4. Chill the cake pops in refrigerator (for about 15 minutes).

5. Remove the cake pops from the refrigerator. Dip a cake pop into the candy coating. Once completely covered, gently pull the cake pop out and gently tap the stick on the edge of the bowl to allow the excess candy coating to drip off. Place in a stand.

6. As the pop hardens, but is still slightly soft, coat the cake pop with the green sugar sprinkles while holding it over a bowl. Place in stand and let dry completely. Repeat steps 5 and 6 with remaining cake pops.

7. With the black edible color pen, draw a small circle on top of the flat surface of each of the green candy coating wafers that have been reserved for the putting green decorations.

8. Dip the tip of a toothpick into the candy coating and dab on top of a cake pop. Gently press the rounded side of a green candy coating wafer against it so the flat side faces up. Hold until it is securely fastened to the cake pop. Repeat with remaining cake pops.

9. Dip the tip of a toothpick into the candy coating and dab onto the top of the flat surface where the golf ball will be positioned. Attach the white dragée sprinkle for the golf ball. Repeat with remaining cake pops.

10. Make the flags: Cut red cardstock paper into 2" diamonds. Put a line of glue down the middle of the diamond with a glue stick. Fold the paper around the top of a toothpick. Stick the toothpick into a cake pop, just behind the hole. Repeat with remaining cake pops.

11. Let pops stand and dry completely.

MAKES 24 CAKE POPS

These cake pops will make a big splash!

WHAT YOU'LL NEED

24 uncoated round cake balls
1 14- or 16-oz. bag blue candy coating
24 lollipop sticks
4 oz. vanilla wafer cookies (crushed)
4 oz. orange candy coating
4 oz. white candy coating
1 to 2 oz. pink candy coating (small handful)
3 4-oz. squeeze bottles
Flip-flop candy mold

WHAT TO DO

1. Prepare the uncoated round cake balls *(see basic pop recipe on page 21)*.

2. Place the blue candy coating in a microwave-safe bowl. Melt in the microwave, following the instructions on the package. Stir until you get a smooth consistency.

3. Dip the tip of a lollipop stick into the blue candy coating about a half inch. Insert dipped end of stick into a cake ball, about halfway through the ball.

Place ball on a plate or cookie sheet lined with wax paper. Repeat with remaining cake balls.

4. Chill the cake pops in refrigerator (for about 15 minutes).

5. Remove the cake pops from the refrigerator. Dip a cake pop into the blue candy coating. Once completely covered, pull the cake pop out and gently tap the stick on the edge of the bowl to allow the excess candy coating to drip off. Place in a stand.

6. As the pop hardens, but is still slightly soft, sprinkle the cake pop with the crushed vanilla wafer crumbs while holding it over a bowl. Place in stand and let dry completely. Repeat steps 5 and 6 with remaining cake pops.

7. Place the orange, white, and pink candy coating into separate microwave-safe bowls. Melt in the microwave, following the instructions on the package. Stir until you get a smooth consistency.

8. Create the starfish: Pour the orange candy coating into a squeeze bottle. Gently draw stars on wax paper to create a starfish. Repeat to create 12 starfish in total. Let dry until completely hardened. Remove by gently peeling away from the wax paper and set aside.

9. Create the flip-flops: Pour the white and pink candy coating into separate squeeze bottles. With the flip-flop candy mold, you will first gently fill in the straps of the sandals with the pink candy coating. Fill 12 pairs of flip-flop straps. Let dry completely. Fill in the rest of each sandal with the white candy coating, filling over the pink strap and to the top. Once all are filled, hold both sides of the mold and tap it lightly on the tabletop. This will level out the chocolate and remove any air bubbles. Place the mold in the refrigerator for five minutes to harden. Take the mold out and turn it upside down. Gently tap it on the table and the candy flip-flops should drop right out. Set them aside.

10. Dip the tip of a toothpick into the blue candy coating and dab onto the top of a cake pop. Attach either a starfish or a pair of flip-flops on top. Repeat with remaining cake pops.

11. Let pops stand and dry completely.

TIPS

• Starfish could also be made from fondant using a small star-shaped cutter.

• Stick margarita umbrellas in the cake pops to give them added beach flair!

BLOWFISH

MAKES 24 CAKE POPS

Cast your line and catch a blowfish cake pop!

WHAT YOU'LL NEED

24 uncoated round cake balls
1 14- or 16-oz. bag blue candy coating
1 14- or 16-oz. bag yellow candy coating
24 lollipop sticks
16 blue candy coating wafers (reserve for fin & tail decorations)
16 yellow candy coating wafers (reserve for fin & tail decorations)
48 candy eyes
12 jumbo red heart sprinkles
4 oz. orange candy coating

WHAT TO DO

1. Prepare the uncoated round cake balls *(see basic pop recipe on page 21)*.

2. Place the bags of blue and yellow candy coating into separate microwave-safe bowls. Melt in the microwave, following the instructions on the package. Stir until you get a smooth consistency.

3. In this recipe I am suggesting you create 12 blue and 12 yellow blowfish cake pops, though, of course, you

could do all the same or any variety that you'd like. Dip the tip of a lollipop stick into the blue or yellow candy coating about a half inch. Insert dipped end of stick into a cake ball, about halfway through the ball. Place ball on a plate or cookie sheet lined with wax paper. Repeat with remaining cake balls.

4. Chill the cake pops in refrigerator (for about 15 minutes).

5. Create the fins: Cut 4 of the blue candy coating wafers, and 4 of the yellow candy coating wafers, in half using a knife. Then, cut each half into 3 equal triangle pieces. You should be able to make 6 fins from one candy coating wafer. Repeat to create 24 fins and set aside.

6. Create the tails: With the remaining 24 candy coating wafers (12 blue, 12 yellow), trim off the edges and create triangles the width of the candy wafer. One candy wafer will make 1 tail. Set the 24 tails aside.

7. Remove the cake pops from the refrigerator. Dip a cake pop into the blue or yellow candy coating. Once completely covered, pull the cake pop out and gently tap the stick on the edge of the bowl to allow the excess candy coating to drip off. Place in a stand.

8. As the pop hardens, but is still slightly soft, attach the candy eyes. Attach a heart sprinkle for the mouth by gently inserting the pointed end of the

heart into the front of the cake pop. Attach the tail by gently inserting the pointed end of the candy wafer into the back of the cake pop. Place in stand and let dry completely. Repeat steps 7 and 8 with remaining cake pops.

9. Dip the tip of a toothpick into the blue or yellow candy coating and dab onto the sides where the fins will be positioned. Attach one fin on each side of a cake pop and let dry completely. Repeat with remaining cake pops.

10. Place the orange candy coating in a microwave-safe bowl. Melt in the microwave, following the instructions on the package. Stir until you get a smooth consistency.

11. Dip the tip of a toothpick into the orange candy coating and dot onto a cake pop lifting up in a short, quick motion to create a spike. Repeat to create spikes all over the fish. Repeat with remaining cake pops.

12. Let pops stand and dry completely.

TIPS

• The spikes can also be created by using a squeeze bottle.

• Create texture on the tail and fins by dipping a toothpick into the orange candy coating and drawing extra lines on the fins and tail.

COCKTAILS
MARGARITAS & MARTINIS

MAKES 24 CAKE POPS

*It's happy hour somewhere in the world right now . . .
start it off right with a cocktail cake pop!*

WHAT YOU'LL NEED

24 uncoated cake cones *(shaping instructions below)*
1 14- or 16-oz. bag green candy coating
1 14- or 16-oz. bag pink candy coating
24 lollipop sticks
1 14- or 16-oz. bag white candy coating
24 white candy coating wafers
    (reserve for "glass" bottom decoration)
Sugar sprinkles
6 green candy coating wafers
    (reserve for lime decoration)
12 toothpicks
12 black or green jelly beans

WHAT TO DO

1. Prepare the uncoated cake cones by first rolling out
    all of the individual balls for the basic cake pops
    (see page 21). Then place a ball in the palm of your
    hand. Roll the ball between both of your hands to
    create a pointed end. Flatten the opposite end on
    the counter top. Repeat with remaining cake balls

and place them all on a plate or cookie sheet lined with wax paper.

2. Place the green and pink candy coating in separate microwave-safe bowls. Melt in the microwave, following the instructions on the package. Stir until you get a smooth consistency.

3. In this recipe I am suggesting you create 12 green margarita and 12 pink martini cake pops, though, of course, you could do all the same or any variety that you'd like. Dip the tip of a lollipop stick into the green or pink candy coating about a half inch. Insert dipped end of stick into the pointed end of a cake cone, making sure it is inserted far enough to achieve stability. Place cone on a plate or cookie sheet lined with wax paper. Repeat with remaining cake cones.

4. Chill the cake pops in refrigerator (for about 15 minutes).

5. Remove the cake pops from the refrigerator. Dip a cake pop into the green or pink candy coating. Once completely covered, pull the cake pop out and gently tap the stick on the edge of the bowl to allow the excess candy coating to drip off. Place in a stand and let dry completely. Repeat with remaining cake pops.

6. Place the bag of white candy coating into a microwave-safe bowl. Melt in the microwave, following the instructions on the package. Stir until you get a smooth consistency.

7. Dip the top portion of a cake pop into the white candy coating. Hold upside down and gently tap to let the excess drip off. Place in a stand and let dry completely. Repeat with remaining cake pops.

8. Create the "glass" bottoms using the reserved 24 white candy coating wafers. Use the sharp end of a bamboo skewer (or anything sharp) to poke a hole in the center of the candy wafer. Gently slide it through the bottom of the lollipop stick and position about an inch below the base of the pop. If it slips, you can dip the tip of a toothpick into the melted white candy coating and dab in between the

base of the wafer and the lollipop stick. Repeat with remaining cake pops.

9. To create the margaritas: Dip the tip of a toothpick into the white candy coating. Lightly coat the edge of the rim of a green cake pop. Pour the sugar sprinkles over the rim. Repeat with remaining green cake pops. Cut each of the 6 green candy coating wafers (that have been reserved for the lime decorations), in half with a knife. Dip the tip of a toothpick into the white candy coating and dab onto the rim of the cake pop where you will attach the lime. Hold the candy wafer "lime" in place until secure. Dip the tip of a toothpick into the white candy coating and draw on the lines of the lime wedge. Repeat for remaining green pops.

10. To create the martinis: Poke the toothpick through a jelly bean about halfway. Stick one end into the top of a pink cake pop toward the edge. Repeat with remaining pink cake pops.

11. Let stand and dry completely.

PIÑA COLADAS

MAKES 24 CAKE POPS

Bring a luau to your own backyard with these stylish and adorable piña colada cake pops!

WHAT YOU'LL NEED

24 uncoated cake coconut cups *(shaping instructions below)*
1 14- or 16-oz. bag milk chocolate candy coating
24 lollipop sticks
4 yellow candy coating wafers
24 red crunch sprinkles
1 teaspoon light corn syrup
Food-safe paintbrush
White nonpareils
24 mini umbrellas

WHAT TO DO

1. Prepare the uncoated cake coconut cups by first rolling out all of the individual balls for the basic cake pops *(see page 21)*. Then place each ball on wax paper and flatten one side of the ball push-

ing against the counter. This will be the top of the

coconut cup shape. Place them all on a plate or cookie sheet lined with wax paper.

2. Place the milk chocolate candy coating in a microwave-safe bowl. Melt in the microwave, following the instructions on the package. Stir until you get a smooth consistency.

3. Dip the tip of a lollipop stick into the milk chocolate candy coating about a half inch. Insert that end of the stick into the bottom of a cake coconut cup, making sure it is inserted far enough to achieve stability. Place on a plate or cookie sheet lined with wax paper. Repeat with remaining cake coconut cups.

4. Chill the cake pops in refrigerator (for about 15 minutes).

5. Create the pineapple wedges: Cut the 4 yellow candy coating wafers in half using a knife. Then, cut each half into 3 equal triangle pieces. You should be able to make 6 wedges from one candy coating wafer. Repeat to create 24 total wedges. Set aside.

6. Remove the cake pops from the refrigerator. Dip a cake pop into the milk chocolate candy coating. Once completely covered, pull the cake pop out and gently tap the stick on the edge of the bowl to

allow the excess candy coating to drip off. Place in a stand.

7. As the chocolate hardens, but is still slightly soft, texture the side of the pop by gently dragging a toothpick up and down the sides of the ball to create the coconut shell effect.

8. As the chocolate continues to harden, attach one of the yellow triangle wedges on the edge of the flat surface of the pop. Attach the red chocolate crunch sprinkle next to it. (Dab the tip of a toothpick into the chocolate coating and use as "glue" if needed, to attach the wedge and sprinkle.) This will create the look of a pineapple and cherry. Repeat steps 6 through 8 with the remaining cake pops.

9. Pour the light corn syrup into a small bowl. Using a food-safe paintbrush, gently brush a small amount of the light corn syrup onto the flat surface of a cake pop. While holding the cake pop over a bowl, sprinkle the white nonpareils over the top until covered. Repeat with remaining cake pops.

10. Stick a mini umbrella into the top of each of the cake pops.

11. Let pops stand and dry completely.

TIPS

- A thin layer of melted chocolate candy coating could be used in place of the light corn syrup.

- It's also fun to insert a small piece of sour straw candy on top to look like a straw for the piña colada.

SPECIALTY FLAVORS

• • • • • • • • • • • •

It's time to think outside the "box" . . . boxed cake that is! There are so many different things you can do with these tiny desserts—the possibilities are endless. Now is the time to let your creativity take over and your taste buds do the talking. Have fun experimenting with different flavor extracts, candy, and nut combinations.

I've included some recipes to get you started on taking these bite-sized pops in a different direction. You'll find the perfect combination of sweet and savory with **Peanut** cake pops, and discover a new campfire classic with quick and easy **S'mores** pops. You'll also love turning an everyday cheesecake into exciting **Cheesecake** pops and putting a new spin on the classic **Cherry Pie**!

Have Fun with Extracts!

A little bit of store-bought extract will go a long way and will give each cake pop an added kick. As you melt candy coating, stir in your favorite extracts. Start with a few drops and add more until you get the flavor you're looking for. Adding a little bit of lemon extract into your candy coating makes for a wonderful combination. Try adding mint extract into your melted chocolate for a delightfully fresh pairing.

Mix it Up!

While a boxed cake mix might offer the most consistent and predictable results, don't let your imagination stop there. Feel free to chop, grind, or crush up your favorite ingredients. As you mix the cake with the frosting to create the cake pop ball, stir in anything you'd like—from crushed up candy to nuts. Start with one cup of your favorite mix-ins and add more until you get your desired consistency. Peanuts or walnuts are always great, or crush up your favorite candy bar to give your cake pops that personalized touch!

PEANUT CAKE POPS

MAKES 24 CAKE POPS

You'll go nuts for these peanut pops!

WHAT YOU'LL NEED

24 uncoated round peanut cake balls *(see mixing instructions below)*
1-1/2 cups crushed peanuts, divided
1 14- or 16-oz. bag milk chocolate candy coating
24 lollipop sticks

HOW TO MIX

When mixing the cake with the frosting for the basic cake pops *(see page 21)*, stir in 1 cup of the crushed peanuts. After the cake reaches the desired consistency, continue to roll out the individual balls and place them all on a plate or cookie sheet lined with wax paper.

WHAT TO DO

1. Place the candy coating in a microwave-safe bowl. Melt in the microwave, following the instructions on the package. Stir until you get a smooth consistency.

2. Dip the tip of a lollipop stick into the candy coating about a half inch. Insert dipped end of stick into a cake ball, about halfway through the ball.

Place ball on a plate or cookie sheet lined with wax paper. Repeat with remaining cake balls.

3. Chill the cake pops in refrigerator (for about 15 minutes).

4. Remove the cake pops from the refrigerator. Dip a cake pop into the candy coating. Once completely covered, pull the cake pop out and gently tap the stick on the edge of the bowl to allow the excess candy coating to drip off. Place in a stand.

5. As the chocolate coating hardens, but is still slightly soft, sprinkle the remaining 1/2 cup of crushed peanuts all over the chocolate coated cake pop while holding over a bowl. Place in stand. Repeat steps 4 and 5 with remaining cake pops.

6. Let pops stand and dry completely.

TIPS

• To give these cake pops an added peanut kick, use peanut butter as the binder instead of frosting.

• You can also use peanut butter-flavored candy coating for the base, and drizzle melted chocolate over the top as seen in the picture.

S'MORES POPS

MAKES 24 POPS

Enjoy a campfire classic with a new twist!

WHAT YOU'LL NEED

1 14- or 16-oz. bag milk chocolate candy coating
24 jumbo marshmallows
24 lollipop sticks
1-1/2 cups crushed graham crackers

WHAT TO DO

1. Place the candy coating in a microwave-safe bowl. Melt in the microwave, following the instructions on the package. Stir until you get a smooth consistency.

2. Insert a lollipop stick into one end of a marshmallow, about halfway through.

3. Dip the marshmallow straight down into the candy coating, until about half of it is covered. Carefully pull the marshmallow out and gently tap the stick on the edge of the bowl to allow the excess candy coating to drip off. Place in a stand.

4. As the chocolate coating hardens, but is still slightly soft, sprinkle the crushed graham crackers over the

melted chocolate. Place in a stand. Repeat steps 2 through 4 with remaining marshmallows.

5. Let pops stand and dry completely.

TIP

• Have fun experimenting with colored marshmallows!

CHEESECAKE POPS

MAKES 18 POPS

Turn an everyday cheesecake into delicious cheesecake pops!

WHAT YOU'LL NEED

9" store-bought cheesecake (chilled)
Cookie scoop
2 cups crushed graham crackers
1 14- or 16-oz. bag milk chocolate candy coating
18 lollipop sticks

WHAT TO DO

1. Use the cookie scoop to make the balls out of the cheesecake. Continue to scoop balls until all of the cheesecake is gone. You should be able to get about 18 balls. Place all the balls on a plate or cookie sheet lined with wax paper.

2. Pour the crushed graham crackers into a cake pan. Roll each cheesecake ball in the graham cracker crumbs until completely coated, working quickly. Place on a plate or cookie sheet lined with wax paper and refrigerate.

3. Place the candy coating in a microwave-safe bowl. Melt in the microwave, following the instructions on the package. Stir until you get a smooth consistency.

4. Dip the tip of a lollipop stick into the candy coating about a half inch. Insert dipped end of stick into the cheesecake ball, about halfway through the ball. Place ball on a plate or cookie sheet lined with wax paper. Repeat with remaining cheesecake balls.

5. Chill the cheesecake pops in the refrigerator for 30 minutes to let harden.

6. Remove the cake pops from the refrigerator. (You may need to re-melt the candy coating.) Dip the cheesecake pop into the candy coating. Once completely covered, pull the cheesecake pop out and gently tap the stick on the edge of the bowl to allow the excess candy coating to drip off. Place in a stand and repeat with remaining pops.

7. Let pops stand and dry completely. Refrigerate after completion and prior to serving.

TIP

- Coating the cheesecake in the graham cracker crumbs helps the ball hold its shape. You'll need to work fast with these as the cheesecake will warm up quickly and can be tricky to handle.

CHERRY PIE POPS

MAKES 16–18 PIE POPS

Take a break from the cake and enjoy a pie pop instead!

WHAT YOU'LL NEED

1 box of store-bought pie crusts, softened as directed
   on the box
3" round cookie cutter
16–18 lollipop sticks
10 oz. store-bought cherry pie filling
1 egg, beaten
16–18 strands of pink ribbon (about 7" each)

WHAT TO DO

1. Preheat oven to 425°F. Spray a cookie sheet with
    cooking spray.

2. Unroll the pie crusts onto a flat work surface. Cut
    32 to 36 round circles with the cookie cutter.

3. Place about 12 pie circles on the cookie sheet.
    Leave about 1" in between each circle.

4. Gently press a lollipop stick into the center of a
    round crust. Place about 1 teaspoon of pie filling
    in the center of the crust. (This is about two cher-
    ries with just a little bit of the extra juices.) Cover
    with a second pie circle. Using an extra lollipop

stick or a fork, press around the edges to seal it closed. Repeat with remaining circles.

5. Using a pastry brush, lightly brush the surface of each of the pie pops with the beaten egg.

6. Bake for 15 minutes or until golden brown. Place on a cooling rack and let cool completely.

7. Tie a ribbon around the lollipop stick at the base of the pie, and repeat with remaining pie pops.

TIPS

• Store-bought pie filling often comes in 21 oz. cans. Half of a can will be more than enough for one recipe.

• After cutting the round circles for the pie crusts, the leftover dough can be rolled back up into a ball and flattened out to create more rounds.

• You can use any kind of filling to create the pie pop flavor of your choice. Use pumpkin pie filling and mix it up at Thanksgiving!

MEASUREMENT & TEMPERATURE EQUIVALENTS

• • • • • • • • • • •

U.S. LIQUID/ DRY MEASURES	OUNCES	METRIC
1 teaspoon	0.16	5 ml
1 tablespoon	0.5	15 ml
1 ounce	1.0	30 ml
1/4 cup	2.0	57 ml
1/2 cup	4.0	118 ml
1 cup	16.0	237 ml

TEMPERATURE

FAHRENHEIT	CELSIUS
350°	180°
425°	220°

LENGTHS

U.S.	METRIC
1/8 inch	3.175 mm
1/4 inch	6.35 mm
1/2 inch	12.7 mm
1 inch	2.5 cm

ABOUT POP.O.LiCiOUS CAKE POPS

• • • • • • • • • • • • •

Pop.O.Licious Cake Pops was founded in late 2010 by Joey and Tony Dellino of Seattle, WA. It started as an outlet for Joey to express her creativity through cake pops, with the vision of one day selling them locally. It quickly led to the two of them expanding their company through the world of blogging and social media. In February 2011, their cake pop blog, **Every Day Should Pop!** *(www.365cakepops.com)* was created as an extension to the Pop.O.Licious brand. **Every Day Should Pop!** became a popular resource for cake pop enthusiasts and attracted national attention. Joey's cute, clever, and whimsical designs continue to put smiles on the faces of her fans and brighten their days—one Pop.O.Licious cake pop at a time!

www.365cakepops.com

Designed by Heather Zschock

Text and photographs copyright © 2012 Joey Dellino and
Anthony Dellino

Photos courtesy of Shutterstock Images as follows:

p. 10: © Elina Manninen
p. 25: © Margoe Edwards
p. 75: © GrigoryL
p. 83: © pick
p. 87: © Zuzanae
p. 147: © Alkestida
p. 177: © Ruggiero.S
p. 186: © Sandra van der Steen

Copyright © 2012
Peter Pauper Press, Inc
202 Mamaroneck Avenue
White Plains, NY 10601
All rights reserved
ISBN 978-1-4413-1018-7
Printed in Hong Kong

7 6 5 4 3 2

Visit us at www.peterpauper.com